Economic Growth

NATIONAL BUREAU OF ECONOMIC RESEARCH

General Series 96

Economic Research: Retrospect and Prospect

ECONOMIC GROWTH

Fiftieth Anniversary Colloquium V

NATIONAL BUREAU OF ECONOMIC RESEARCH
NEW YORK 1972

Distributed by COLUMBIA UNIVERSITY PRESS
NEW YORK AND LONDON

Relation of National Bureau Directors to Publications
Reporting Proceedings of the Fiftieth Anniversary Colloquia

Since the present volume is a record of colloquium proceedings, it has been exempted from the rules governing submission of manuscripts to, and critical review by, the Board of Directors of the National Bureau. *(Resolution adopted July 6, 1948, as revised November 21, 1949, and April 20, 1968)*

Prefatory Note

This volume of the Fiftieth Anniversary Series contains the proceedings of the Economic Growth Colloquium, which was held at the Bank of America Center in San Francisco, California, on December 10, 1970. We are indebted to those members of the Bureau's Board of Directors who served on the committee to plan and coordinate the session: Moses Abramovitz, Percival F. Brundage, Solomon Fabricant, Frank W. Fetter, Walter D. Fisher, David L. Grove, Harold G. Halcrow, John R. Meyer, Douglass C. North, Robert M. Solow, and Joseph H. Willits. In addition, the splendid assistance received from Bureau director Walter E. Hoadley merits our special appreciation. He obtained the facilities and contributed substantial time and effort to ensuring the success of the Economic Growth Colloquium. Finally, we are grateful to Ester Moskowitz, Hedy D. Jellinek, and Ruth Ridler, who prepared the manuscript for publication.

F. Thomas Juster

Fiftieth Anniversary Colloquium Series

To commemorate its fiftieth anniversary the National Bureau of Economic Research sponsored a series of colloquia to explore the effects of pending and anticipated policy issues on future research priorities for areas of long-standing Bureau concern. As a basis for the panel and audience discussions, economists specializing in the subject area prepared papers in which they reviewed relevant research advances through time and presented their opinions for the direction of future effort. These papers, and in some instances edited transcripts of panelists' comments, appear as part of the National Bureau's Fiftieth Anniversary publications series. Papers developed for the colloquia and publications series and participants in the program included:

THE BUSINESS CYCLE TODAY
September 24, 1970—New York City

Moderators:
> Morning session: Paul A. Samuelson
> Afternoon session: F. Thomas Juster

Presentations:
> "Dating American Growth Cycles"   *Ilse Mintz*
> "The 'Recession' of 1969–1970"   *Solomon Fabricant*
> "The Cyclical Behavior of Prices"   *Geoffrey H. Moore*
> "Forecasting Economic Conditions: The Record and the Prospect"
> *Victor Zarnowitz*
> "Econometric Model Simulations and the Cyclical Characteristics
> of the U.S. Economy"   *Victor Zarnowitz*
> "A Study of Discretionary and Nondiscretionary Monetary and
> Fiscal Policies in the Context of Stochastic Macroeconometric
> Models"   *Yoel Haitovsky and Neil Wallace*

Panelists:
Morning session: Otto Eckstein, Henry C. Wallich
Afternoon session: Bert G. Hickman, Arthur M. Okun

FINANCE AND CAPITAL MARKETS
October 22, 1970—New York City

Moderator: Robert V. Roosa

Presentation:
"Finance and Capital Markets"   *John Lintner*

Panelists: William J. Baumol, Sidney Homer, James J. O'Leary

A ROUNDTABLE ON POLICY ISSUES AND RESEARCH OPPORTUNITIES IN INDUSTRIAL ORGANIZATION
November 5, 1970—Chicago, Illinois

Moderator: Victor R. Fuchs

Presentations:
"Industrial Organization: Boxing the Compass"
       James W. McKie
"Antitrust Enforcement and the Modern Corporation"
       Oliver E. Williamson
"Issues in the Study of Industrial Organization in a Regime of Rapid
  Technical Change"   *Richard R. Nelson*
"Industrial Organization: A Proposal for Research"
       Ronald H. Coase

PUBLIC EXPENDITURES AND TAXATION
December 2, 1970—Washington, D.C.

Moderator: Walter W. Heller

Presentation:
"Quantitative Research in Taxation and Government Expenditure"
Carl S. Shoup
Panelists: James M. Buchanan, Richard R. Musgrave

ECONOMIC GROWTH
December 10, 1970—San Francisco, California

Moderator: R. Aaron Gordon

Presentation:
"Is Growth Obsolete?"
William D. Nordhaus and James Tobin

Panelists: Moses Abramovitz, Robin C. O. Matthews

HUMAN RESOURCES
May 13, 1971—Atlanta, Georgia

Moderator: Gary S. Becker

Presentation:
"Human Capital: Policy Issues and Research Opportunities"
Theodore W. Schultz

Panelists: Alice M. Rivlin, Gerald S. Somers

THE FUTURE OF ECONOMIC RESEARCH
April 23, 1971—South Brookline, Massachusetts

Presentation:

"Quantitative Economic Research: Trends and Problems"

Simon Kuznets

Contents

FOREWORD   F. Thomas Juster   xv

IS GROWTH OBSOLETE?   William Nordhaus   1
                                James Tobin

DISCUSSION   81

Foreword

Whether the difference between economic growth as measured by the present U.S. National Income and Product Accounts and economic growth as measured by a welfare-oriented and fully comprehensive set of economic accounts is large or small — indeed, whether welfare-oriented growth has been positive or negative during the last decade or so — has received a great deal of both public and professional attention of late. Some have presented the extreme view that there has been no real economic growth at all in the U.S. economy over the recent past, as the apparent growth in measured product has been eaten away by an increasingly important set of negative growth elements manifested by a massive deterioration in our physical and social environment.

The critics may be right or wrong, but they have certainly made the point that our Income and Product Accounts do not provide a measure of economic and social welfare, and that they may give a seriously misleading picture of the growth in welfare. The appropriate response to the critics, and to the questions they pose, does not lie in verbal and empirically casual counter-arguments. It consists, rather, in an attempt to adjust, modify, and supplement the Income and Product Accounts for the kinds of welfare-producing activities, both positive and negative, that are either not included as part of real product or are included as final rather than intermediate product. The essay by William Nordhaus and James Tobin represents the first serious quantitative attempt to do this, and to provide a comprehensive measure of output that is welfare-oriented rather than production- or activity-oriented.

The latter difference is important. An expansion in real product which takes the form of more police, fire, and other protective services, or greater military hardware and personnel, or a larger fleet of garbage removal trucks clearly represents increased output in the sense that a greater flow of resources are used for these purposes by the community. But if these expanded flows of product do no more than simply maintain existing "stocks" of personal security, national security, and ecological purity, it is hard to see where economic welfare has been increased by this expanded use of real resources. The problem is thorny, especially on the measurement side, since it is ordinarily far from obvious whether increased product flows of the sort described above have or have not resulted in greater amounts of the ultimate services they are designed to provide. For example, have we really purchased more personal and national security by our expanded outlays?

An identical problem arises with respect to the role of nonmarket activities in the system. An expansion of leisure time is generally regarded as a positive economic and social benefit. An increase in the utility associated with work, including a better-regulated physical environment due to improved heating, lighting, and ventilation, as well as a more attractive work situation itself are surely positive economic benefits. And a change in the composition of nonworking time, away from the drudgery of household chores and toward activities like television viewing, reading, visiting the neighbors, or whatever, is just as much an increase in leisure time as a reduction in the number of hours spent working for pay.

Nordhaus and Tobin make an imaginative attempt to quantify some of the important differences between the concept of goods and services produced in the market and the welfare concept of goods and services available for ultimate consumption satisfactions. Their calculations suggest that the extensively discussed and debated gaps in the accounts data relating to the growth in environmental disamenities (pollution, urban crises, racial disharmony, etc.), while sizable in absolute terms, play a relatively modest role in the total picture when compared with other gaps that are both positive and negative. Not surprisingly, the most important single difference between welfare and production turns out to be in the value of leisure time, although there are very large differences in alternative ways of valuing the growth in available leisure.

It is easy to quarrel with the specifics of the Nordhaus-Tobin quantitative estimate of measured welfare or of its growth over time. But the authors' contribution lies less in their specific measurements (provided in a tentative and qualified form) than in their demonstration of the fact that sensible measurements *can* be made of an output concept more closely associated with welfare than the production concept characterizing our present Income and Product Accounts.

An interesting footnote relates to their analysis of environmental disamenity. First, quantitative estimates of the costs of environmental deterioration suggest that these costs may not be as large as the more vocal critics of economic growth have usually implied. Second, and more important, Nordhaus and Tobin suggest that the most significant aspect of the environmental problem probably does not lie in the "local" types of disturbances that get so much public attention, such as air and water pollution, crime rates in the cities, etc., but in the potentially catastrophic global ecological disasters that neither the physical sciences nor the social sciences seem to know very much about.

F. THOMAS JUSTER
Vice President — Research

Economic Growth

Is Growth Obsolete?

William Nordhaus and James Tobin

Yale University

A long decade ago economic growth was the reigning fashion of political economy. It was simultaneously the hottest subject of economic
theory and research, a slogan eagerly claimed by politicians of all
stripes, and a serious objective of the policies of governments. The
climate of opinion has changed dramatically. Disillusioned critics indict
both economic science and economic policy for blind obeisance to aggregate material "progress," and for neglect of its costly side effects.
Growth, it is charged, distorts national priorities, worsens the distribution of income, and irreparably damages the environment. Paul Erlich
speaks for a multitude when he says, "We must acquire a life style
which has as its goal maximum freedom and happiness for the individual, not a maximum Gross National Product."

Growth was in an important sense a discovery of economics after
the Second World War. Of course economic development has always
been the grand theme of historically minded scholars of large mind and
bold concept, notably Marx, Schumpeter, Kuznets. But the mainstream
of economic analysis was not comfortable with phenomena of change
and progress. The stationary state was the long-run equilibrium of
classical and neoclassical theory, and comparison of alternative static
equilibriums was the most powerful theoretical tool. Technological
change and population increase were most readily accommodated as
one-time exogenous shocks; comparative static analysis could be used
to tell how they altered the equilibrium of the system. The obvious fact
that these "shocks" were occurring continuously, never allowing the

Note: We would like to express our appreciation to Walter Dolde, James Pugash,
Geoffrey Woglom, Hugh Tobin, and especially Laura Harrison, for assistance in the
preparation of this paper. We are grateful to Robin Matthews for pointing out some
problems in our treatment of leisure in the first draft.

system to reach its equilibrium, was a considerable embarrassment. Keynesian theory fell in the same tradition, attempting rather awkwardly, though nonetheless fruitfully, to apply static equilibrium theory to the essentially dynamic problem of saving and capital accumulation.

Sir Roy Harrod in 1940 began the process, brought to fruition by many theorists in the 1950s, of putting the stationary state into motion. The long-run equilibrium of the system became a path of steady growth, and the tools of comparative statics could then be applied to alternative growth paths rather than to alternative stationary states. Neo-Keynesian macroeconomics began to fall into place as a description of departures from equilibrium growth, although this task of reinterpretation and integration is still far from a satisfactory completion.

By now modern neoclassical growth theory is well enough formulated to have made its way into textbooks. It is a theory of the growth of potential output, or output at a uniform standard rate of utilization of capacity. The theory relates potential output to three determinants: the labor force, the state of technology, and the stock of human and tangible capital. The first two are usually assumed to grow smoothly at rates determined exogenously by noneconomic factors. The accumulation of capital is governed by the thrift of the population, and in equilibrium the growth of the capital stock matches the growth of labor-*cum*-technology and the growth of output. Simple as it is, the model fits the observed trends of economic growth reasonably well.

The steady equilibrium growth of modern neoclassical theory is, it must be acknowledged, a routine process of replication. It is a dull story compared to the convulsive structural, technological, and social changes described by the historically oriented scholars of development mentioned above. The theory conceals, either in aggregation or in the abstract generality of multisector models, all the drama of the events —the rise and fall of products, technologies, and industries, and the accompanying transformations of the spatial and occupational distribution of the population. Many economists agree with the broad outlines of Schumpeter's vision of capitalist development, which is a far cry from growth models made nowadays in either Cambridge, Massachusetts, or Cambridge, England. But visions of that kind have yet to be transformed into a theory that can be applied in everyday analytic and empirical work.

In any case, growth of some kind is now the recognized economic norm. A symptom of the change in outlook can be found in business cycle semantics. A National Bureau *recession* was essentially a period in which aggregate productive activity was declining. Since 1960 it has become increasingly customary to describe the state of the economy by the gap between its actual output and its growing potential. Although the word recession is still a source of confusion and controversy, almost everyone recognizes that the economy is losing ground —which will have to be recaptured eventually—whenever its actual rate of expansion is below the rate of growth of potential output.

In the early 1960s growth became a proclaimed objective of government policy, in this country as elsewhere. Who could be against it? But like most value-laden words, growth has meant different things to different people and at different times. Often growth policy was simply identified with measures to expand aggregate demand in order to bring or keep actual output in line with potential output. In this sense it is simply stabilization policy, only more gap-conscious and growth-conscious than the cycle-smoothing policies of the past.

To economists schooled in postwar neoclassical growth theory, growth policy proper meant something more than this, and more debatable. It meant deliberate effort to speed up the growth of potential output itself, specifically to accelerate the productivity of labor. Growth policy in this meaning was not widely understood or accepted. The neoclassical model outlined above suggested two kinds of policies to foster growth, possibly interrelated: measures that advanced technological knowledge and measures that increased the share of potential output devoted to accumulation of physical or human capital.[1] Another implication of the standard model was that, unless someone could find a way to accelerate technological progress permanently, policy could not raise the rate of growth permanently. One-shot measures would speed up growth temporarily, for years or decades. But once the economy had absorbed these measures, its future growth rate would be limited once again by constraints of labor and technology. The level of its path, however, would be permanently higher than if the policies had not been undertaken.

Growth measures nearly always involve diversions of current resources from other uses, sacrifices of current consumption for the benefit of succeeding generations of consumers. Enthusiasts for faster

[1] The variety of possible measures, and the difficulty of raising the growth rate by more than one or two percentage points, have been explored by Edward Denison in his influential study, *The Sources of Economic Growth in the United States and the Alternatives Before Us,* New York, Committee for Economic Development, January 1962, Supplementary Paper No. 13.

growth are advocates of the future against the present. Their case rests on the view that in a market economy left to itself, the future would be shortchanged because too small a fraction of current output would be saved. We mention this point now because we shall return later to the ironical fact that the antigrowth men of the 1970s believe that it is they who represent the claims of a fragile future against a voracious present.

Like the enthusiasts to whom they are a reaction, current critics of growth are disenchanted with both theory and policy, with both the descriptive and the normative implications of the doctrines of the previous decade. The sources of disenchantment are worth considering today, because they indicate agenda for future theoretical and empirical research.

We have chosen to direct our attention to three important problems raised by those who question the desirability and possibility of future growth: (a) How good are measures of output currently used for evaluating the growth of economic welfare? (b) Does the growth process inevitably waste our natural resources? (c) How does the rate of population growth affect economic welfare? In particular, what would be the effect of zero population growth?

MEASURES OF ECONOMIC WELFARE

A major question raised by critics of economic growth is whether we have been growing at all in any meaningful sense. Gross national product statistics cannot give the answers, for GNP is not a measure of economic welfare. Erlich is right in claiming that maximization of GNP is not a proper objective of policy. Economists all know that, and yet their everyday use of GNP as the standard measure of economic performance apparently conveys the impression that they are evangelistic workshipers of GNP.

An obvious shortcoming of GNP is that it is an index of production, not consumption. The goal of economic activity, after all, is consumption. Although this is the central premise of economics, the profession has been slow to develop, either conceptually or statistically, a measure of economic performance oriented to consumption, broadly defined and carefully calculated. We have constructed a primitive and experimental "measure of economic welfare" (MEW), in which we attempt to allow for the more obvious discrepancies between GNP and economic welfare. A complete account is given in Appendix A. The main results will be discussed here and summarized in Tables 1 and 2.

In proposing a welfare measure, we in no way deny the importance of the conventional national income accounts or of the output measures based upon them. Our MEW is largely a rearrangement of items of the national accounts. Gross and net national product statistics are the economists' chief tools for short-run analysis, forecasting, and policy and are also indispensable for many other purposes.

Our adjustments to GNP fall into three general categories: reclassification of GNP expenditures as consumption, investment, and intermediate; imputation for the services of consumer capital, for leisure, and for the product of household work; correction for some of the disamenities of urbanization.

1. Reclassification of GNP Final Expenditures

Our purposes are first, to subtract some items that are better regarded as instrumental and intermediate than as final output, and second, to allocate all remaining items between consumption and net investment. Since the national accounts do not differentiate among government purchases of goods and services, one of our major tasks will be to split them among the three categories: intermediate, consumption, and net investment. We will also reclassify some private expenditures.

Intermediate products are goods and services whose contributions to present or future consumer welfare are completely counted in the values of other goods and services. To avoid double counting they should not be included in reckoning the net yield of economic activity. Thus all national income accounts reckon as final consumption the bread but not the flour and as capital formation the finished house but not the lumber. The more difficult and controversial issues in assigning items to intermediate or final categories are the following:

Capital Consumption.   The depreciation of capital stocks is a cost of production, and output required to offset the depreciation is intermediate as surely as materials consumed in the productive process. For most purposes, including welfare indexes, NNP is preferable to GNP. Only the difficulties and lags in estimating capital consumption have made GNP the popular statistic.

However, NNP itself fails to treat many durable goods as capital, and counts as final their entire output whether for replacement or accumulation. These elementary points are worth repeating because some of our colleagues are telling the public that economists glorify wasteful "through-put" for its own sake. Focusing on NNP, and accounting for all durables as capital goods, would avoid such foolish paradoxes as the implication that deliberate efforts to make goods more perishable raise national output. We estimate, however, that proper treatment of consumer durables has little quantitative effect (see Table 1, lines 3 and 5).

The other capital consumption adjustments we have made arise from allowing for government capital and for the educational and medical capital embodied in human beings. In effect, we have reclassified education and health expenditures, both public and private, as capital investments.

Growth Requirements.   In principle net national product tells how much consumption the economy could indefinitely sustain. GNP does not tell that; consuming the whole GNP in any year would impair future consumption prospects. But *per capita* rather than aggregate consumption is the welfare objective; neither economists nor other observers would as a rule regard sheer increase in the numbers of people enjoying the same average standard of living as a gain in welfare. Even NNP exaggerates sustainable *per capita* consumption, except in a society with stationary population—another example of the pervasiveness of the "stationary" assumption in the past. Per capita consumption cannot be sustained with zero net investment; the capital stock must be growing at the same rate as population and the labor force. This capital-widening requirement is as truly a cost of staying in the same position as outright capital consumption.[2]

This principle is clear enough when growth is simply increase in population and the labor force. Its application to an economy with technological progress is by no means clear. Indeed, the very concept of national income becomes fuzzy. Should the capital-widening requirement then be interpreted to mean that capital should keep pace with output and technology, not just with the labor force? If so, the implied sustainable consumption per capita grows with the rate of technological progress. This is the point of view which we have taken in what follows. On the other hand, a given level of consumption per capita could be

---

[2] Consider the neoclassical model without technological change. When labor force is growing at rate g, the capital-labor ratio is k, gross product per worker is $f(k)$, net product per worker is $f(k) - \delta k$, then the net investment requirement is gk, and sustainable consumption per worker is $f(k) - \delta k - gk$. Denoting the capital-output ratio as $\mu = [k/f(k)]$, sustainable consumption per worker can also be written as $f(k)[1 - \mu(\delta + g)]$. Although NNP embodies in principle the depreciation deduction δk, it does not take account of the capital-widening requirement gk.

sustained with a steady decline in the capital-output ratio, thanks to technological progress.[3]

The growth requirement is shown on line 7 of Table 2. This is clearly a significant correction, measuring about 16 per cent of GNP in 1965.

Our calculations distinguish between actual and sustainable per capita consumption. *Actual MEW* may exceed or fall short of *sustainable MEW*, the amount that could be consumed while meeting both capital consumption and growth requirements. If these requirements are met, per capita consumption can grow at the trend rate of increase in labor productivity. When actual MEW is less than sustainable MEW, the economy is making even better provision for future consumers; when actual MEW exceeds sustainable MEW, current consumption in effect includes some of the fruits of future progress.

Instrumental Expenditures.   Since GNP and NNP are measures of production rather than of welfare, they count many activities that are evidently not directly sources of utility themselves but are regrettably necessary inputs to activities that may yield utility. Some consumer outlays are only instrumental, for example, the costs of commuting to work. Some government "purchases" are also of this nature—for example, police services, sanitation services, road maintenance, national defense. Expenditures on these items are among the necessary overhead costs of a complex industrial nation-state, although there is plenty of room for disagreement as to the necessary amounts. We are making no judgments on such issues in classifying these outlays as intermediate rather than final uses of resources. Nevertheless, these decisions are difficult and controversial. The issues are clearly illustrated in the important case of national defense.

We exclude defense expenditures for two reasons. First, we see no direct effect of defense expenditures on household economic welfare. No reasonable country (or household) buys "national defense" for its own sake. If there were no war or risk of war, there would be no need

---

[3] As is well known, the whole concept of equilibrium growth collapses unless progress is purely labor-augmenting, "Harrod-neutral." In that case the rate g above is $n + \gamma$, where n is the natural rate of increase and γ is the rate of technological progress, and "labor force" means effective or augmented labor force. In equilibrium, output and consumption per natural worker grow at the rate γ, and "sustainable" consumption per capita means consumption growing steadily at this rate. Clearly, level consumption per capita can be sustained with smaller net investment than $g\mu f(k)$; so μ and k steadily decline. See section A.2.3, below.

for defense expenditures and no one would be the worse without them. Conceptually, then, defense expenditures are gross but not net output.

The second reason is that defense expenditures are input rather than output data. Measurable output is especially elusive in the case of defense. Conceptually, the output of the defense effort is national security. Has the value of the nation's security risen from $0.5 billion to $50 billion over the period from 1929 to 1965? Obviously not. It is patently more reasonable to assume that the rise in expenditure was due to deterioration in international relations and to changes in military technology. The cost of providing a given level of security has risen enormously. If there has been no corresponding gain in security since 1929, the defense cost series is a very misleading indicator of improvements in welfare.

The economy's ability to meet increased defense costs speaks well for its productive performance. But the diversion of productive capacity to this purpose cannot be regarded simply as a shift of national preferences and the product mix. Just as we count technological progress, managerial innovation, and environmental change when they work in our favor (consider new business machines or mineral discoveries) so we must count a deterioration in the environment when it works against us (consider bad weather and war). From the point of view of economic welfare, an arms control or disarmament agreement which would free resources and raise consumption by 10 per cent would be just as significant as new industrial processes yielding the same gains.

In classifying defense costs — or police protection or public health expenditures — as regrettable and instrumental, we certainly do not deny the possibility that given the unfavorable circumstances that prompt these expenditures consumers will ultimately be better off with them than without them. This may or may not be the case. The only judgment we make is that these expenditures yield no direct satisfactions. Even if the "regrettable" outlays are rational responses to unfavorable shifts in the environment of economic activity, we believe that a welfare measure, perhaps unlike a production measure, should record such environmental change.

We must admit, however, that the line between final and instrumental outlays is very hard to draw. For example, the philosophical problems raised by the malleability of consumer wants are too deep to be resolved in economic accounting. Consumers are susceptible to influence by the examples and tastes of other consumers and by the sales efforts of producers. Maybe all our wants are just regrettable necessities; maybe productive activity does no better than to satisfy the wants which it generates; maybe our net welfare product is tautologically zero. More seriously, we cannot measure welfare exclusively by the quantitative flows of goods and services. We need other gauges of the health of individuals and societies. These, too, will be relative to the value systems which determine whether given symptoms indicate health or disease. But the "social indicators" movement of recent years still lacks a coherent, integrative conceptual and statistical framework.

We estimate that overhead and regrettable expenses, so far as we have been able to define and measure them, rose from 8 per cent to 16 per cent of GNP over the period 1929–65 (Table 2, line 4).

2. Imputations for Capital Services, Leisure, and Nonmarket Work

In the national income accounts, rent is imputed on owner-occupied homes and counted as consumption and income. We must make similar imputations in other cases to which we have applied capital accounting. Like owner-occupied homes, other consumer durables and public investments yield consumption directly, without market transactions. In the case of educational and health capital, we have assumed the yields to be intermediate services rather than direct consumption; that is, we expect to see the fruits of investments in education and health realized in labor productivity and earnings, and we do not count them twice. Our measure understates economic welfare and its growth to the extent that education and medical care are direct rather than indirect sources of consumer satisfaction.

The omission of leisure and of nonmarket productive activity from measures of production conveys the impression that economists are blindly materialistic. Economic theory teaches that welfare could rise, even while NNP falls, as the result of voluntary choices to work for pay fewer hours per week, weeks per year, years per lifetime.

These imputations unfortunately raise serious conceptual questions, discussed at some length in section A.3, below. Suppose that in calculating aggregate dollar consumption the hours devoted to leisure and nonmarket productive activity are valued at their presumed opportunity cost, the money wage rate. In converting current dollar consumption to constant dollars, what assumption should be made about the unobservable price indexes for the goods and services consumed during those hours? The wage rate? The price index for marketed con-

TABLE 1

Measures of Economic Welfare, Actual and
Sustainable, Various Years, 1929–65
(*billions of dollars, 1958 prices, except lines 14–19, as noted*)

	1929	1935	1945	1947	1954	1958	1965
1 Personal consumption, national income and product accounts	139.6	125.5	183.0	206.3	255.7	290.1	397.7
2 Private instrumental expenditures	−10.3	−9.2	−9.2	−10.9	−16.4	−19.9	−30.9
3 Durable goods purchases	−16.7	−11.5	−12.3	−26.2	−35.5	−37.9	−60.9
4 Other household investment	−6.5	−6.3	−9.1	−10.4	−15.3	−19.6	−30.1
5 Services of consumer capital imputation	24.9	17.8	22.1	26.7	37.2	40.8	62.3
6 Imputation for leisure							
B	339.5	401.3	450.7	466.9	523.2	554.9	626.9
A	339.5	401.3	450.7	466.9	523.2	554.9	626.9
C	162.9	231.3	331.8	345.6	477.2	554.9	712.8
7 Imputation for nonmarket activities							
B	85.7	109.2	152.4	159.6	211.5	239.7	295.4
A	178.6	189.5	207.1	215.5	231.9	239.7	259.8
C	85.7	109.2	152.4	159.6	211.5	239.7	295.4
8 Disamenity correction	−12.5	−14.1	−18.1	−19.1	−24.3	−27.6	−34.6
9 Government consumption	0.3	0.3	0.4	0.5	0.5	0.8	1.2
10 Services of government capital imputation	4.8	6.4	8.9	10.0	11.7	14.0	16.6
11 Total consumption = actual MEW							
B	548.8	619.4	768.8	803.4	948.3	1,035.3	1,243.6
A	641.7	699.7	823.5	859.3	968.7	1,035.3	1,208.0
C	372.2	449.4	649.9	682.1	902.3	1,035.3	1,329.5
12 MEW net investment	−5.3	−46.0	−52.5	55.3	13.0	12.5	−2.5
13 Sustainable MEW							
B	543.5	573.4	716.3	858.7	961.3	1,047.8	1,241.1
A	636.4	653.7	771.0	914.6	981.7	1,047.8	1,205.5
C	366.9	403.4	597.4	737.4	915.3	1,047.8	1,327.0
14 Population (no. of mill.)	121.8	127.3	140.5	144.7	163.0	174.9	194.6

(*continued*)

Table 1 (concluded)

		1929	1935	1945	1947	1954	1958	1965
	Actual MEW per capita							
15	Dollars							
	B	4,506	4,866	5,472	5,552	5,818	5,919	6,391
	A	5,268	5,496	5,861	5,938	5,943	5,919	6,208
	C	3,056	3,530	4,626	4,714	5,536	5,919	6,832
16	Index (1929 = 100)							
	B	100.0	108.0	121.4	123.2	129.1	131.4	141.8
	A	100.0	104.3	111.3	112.7	112.8	112.4	117.8
	C	100.0	115.5	151.4	154.3	181.2	193.7	223.6
	Sustainable MEW per capita							
17	Dollars							
	B	4,462	4,504	5,098	5,934	5,898	5,991	6,378
	A	5,225	5,135	5,488	6,321	6,023	5,991	6,195
	C	3,012	3,169	4,252	5,096	5,615	5,991	6,819
18	Index (1929 = 100)							
	B	100.0	100.9	114.3	133.0	132.2	134.3	142.9
	A	100.0	98.3	105.0	121.0	115.3	114.7	118.6
	C	100.0	105.2	141.2	169.2	186.4	198.9	226.4
19	Per capita NNP							
	Dollars	1,545	1,205	2,401	2,038	2,305	2,335	2,897
	1929 = 100	100.0	78.0	155.4	131.9	149.2	151.1	187.5

Note: Variants A, B, C in the table correspond to different assumptions about the bearing of technological progress on leisure and nonmarket activities. See section A.3.2, below, for explanation.
Source: Appendix Table A.16.

sumption goods? Over a period of forty years the two diverge substantially; the choice between them makes a big difference in estimates of the growth of MEW. As explained in Appendix A, the market consumption "deflator" should be used if technological progress has augmented nonmarketed uses of time to the same degree as marketed labor. The wage rate should be the deflator if no such progress has occurred in the effectiveness of unpaid time.

In Tables 1 and 2 we provide calculations for three conceptual alternatives. Our own choice is variant B of MEW, in which the value of leisure is deflated by the wage rate; and the value of nonmarket activity, by the consumption deflator.

Economic Research: Retrospect and Prospect

TABLE 2
Gross National Product and MEW, Various Years, 1929–65
(*billions of dollars, 1958 prices*)

	1929	1935	1945	1947	1954	1958	1965
1. Gross national product	203.6	169.5	355.2	309.9	407.0	447.3	617.8
2. Capital consumption, NIPA	−20.0	−20.0	−21.9	−18.3	−32.5	−38.9	−54.7
3. Net national product, NIPA	183.6	149.5	333.3	291.6	374.5	408.4	563.1
4. NIPA final output reclassified as regrettables and intermediates							
a. Government	−6.7	−7.4	−146.3	−20.8	−57.8	−56.4	−63.2
b. Private	−10.3	−9.2	−9.2	−10.9	−16.4	−19.9	−30.9
5. Imputations for items not included in NIPA							
a. Leisure	339.5	401.3	450.7	466.9	523.2	554.9	626.9
b. Nonmarket activity	85.7	109.2	152.4	159.6	211.5	239.7	295.4
c. Disamenities	−12.5	−14.1	−18.1	−19.1	−24.3	−27.6	−34.6
d. Services of public and private capital	29.7	24.2	31.0	36.7	48.9	54.8	78.9
6. Additional capital consumption	−19.3	−33.4	−11.7	−50.8	−35.2	−27.3	−92.7
7. Growth requirement	−46.1	−46.7	−65.8	+5.4	−63.1	−78.9	−101.8
8. Sustainable MEW	543.6	573.4	716.3	858.6	961.3	1,047.7	1,241.1

NIPA = national income and product accounts.

Note: Variants A, B, C in the table correspond to different assumptions about the bearing of technological progress on leisure and nonmarket activities. Variant A assumes that neither has benefited from technological progress at the rate of increase of real wages; variant C assumes that neither has so benefited; variant B assumes that leisure has not been augmented by technological progress but other nonmarket activities have benefited. See section A.3.2, below, for explanation.

Source: Appendix Table A.17.

3. Disamenities of Urbanization

The national income accounts largely ignore the many sources of utility or disutility that are not associated with market transactions or measured by the market value of goods and services. If one of my neighbors cultivates a garden of ever-increasing beauty, and another makes more and more noise, neither my increasing appreciation of the one nor my growing annoyance with the other comes to the attention of the Department of Commerce.

Likewise there are some socially productive assets (for example, the environment) that do not appear in any balance sheets. Their services to producers and consumers are not valued in calculating national income. By the same token no allowance is made for depletion of their capacity to yield services in the future.

Many of the negative "externalities" of economic growth are connected with urbanization and congestion. The secular advances recorded in NNP figures have accompanied a vast migration from rural agriculture to urban industry. Without this occupational and residential revolution we could not have enjoyed the fruits of technological progress. But some portion of the higher earnings of urban residents may simply be compensation for the disamenities of urban life and work. If so we should not count as a gain of welfare the full increments of NNP that result from moving a man from farm or small town to city. The persistent association of higher wages with higher population densities offers one method of estimating the costs of urban life as they are valued by people making residential and occupational decisions.

As explained in section A.4, below, we have tried to estimate by cross-sectional regressions the income differentials necessary to hold people in localities with greater population densities. The resulting estimates of the disamenity costs of urbanization are shown in Table 1, line 8. As can be seen, the estimated disamenity premium is quite substantial, running about 5 per cent of GNP. Nevertheless, the urbanization of the population has not been so rapid that charging it with this cost significantly reduces the estimated rate of growth of the economy.

The adjustments leading from national accounts "personal consumption" to MEW consumption are shown in Table 1, and the relations of GNP, NNP, and MEW are summarized in Table 2. For reasons previously indicated, we believe that a welfare measure should have the dimension *per capita*. We would stress the per capita MEW figures shown in Tables 1 and 2.

Although the numbers presented here are very tentative, they do suggest the following observations. First, MEW is quite different from conventional output measures. Some consumption items omitted from GNP are of substantial quantitative importance. Second, our preferred variant of per capita MEW has been growing more slowly than per capita NNP (1.1 per cent for MEW as against 1.7 per cent for NNP, at annual rates over the period 1929–65). Yet MEW has been growing. The progress indicated by conventional national accounts is not just a myth that evaporates when a welfare-oriented measure is substituted.

GROWTH AND NATURAL RESOURCES

Calculations like the foregoing are unlikely to satisfy critics who believe that economic growth per se piles up immense social costs ignored in even the most careful national income calculations. Faced with the finiteness of our earth and the exponential growth of economy and population, the environmentalist sees inevitable starvation. The specter of Malthus is haunting even the affluent society.

There is a familiar ring to these criticisms. Ever since the industrial revolution pessimistic scientists and economists have warned that the possibilities of economic expansion are ultimately limited by the availability of natural resources and that society only makes the eventual future reckoning more painful by ignoring resource limitations now.

In important part, this is a warning about population growth, which we consider below. Taking population developments as given, will natural resources become an increasingly severe drag on economic growth? We have not found evidence to support this fear. Indeed, the opposite appears to be more likely: Growth of output per capita will accelerate ever so slightly even as stocks of natural resources decline.

The prevailing standard model of growth assumes that there are no limits on the feasibility of expanding the supplies of nonhuman agents of production. It is basically a two-factor model in which production depends only on labor and reproducible capital. Land and resources, the third member of the classical triad, have generally been dropped. The simplifications of theory carry over into empirical work. The thousands of aggregate production functions estimated by econometricians in the last decade are labor-capital functions. Presumably the tacit justification has been that reproducible capital is a near-perfect substitute for land and other exhaustible resources, at least in the perspective of heroic aggregation customary in macroeconomics. If substitution for natural resources is not possible in any given technology, or if a particular resource is exhausted, we tacitly assume that "land-augmenting" innovations will overcome the scarcity.

These optimistic assumptions about technology stand in contrast to the tacit assumption of environmentalists that no substitutes are available for natural resources. Under this condition, it is easily seen that output will indeed stop growing or will decline. It thus appears that the substitutability (or technically, the elasticity of substitution) between the neoclassical factors, capital and labor, and natural resources is of crucial importance to future growth. This is an area needing extensive further research, but we have made two forays to see what the evidence is. Details are given in Appendix B, below.

First we ran several simulations of the process of economic growth in order to see which assumptions about substitution and technology fit the "stylized" facts. The important facts are: growing income per capita and growing capital per capita; relatively declining inputs and income shares of natural resources; and a slowly declining capital-output ratio. Among the various forms of production function considered, the following assumptions come closest to reproducing these stylized facts: (a) Either the elasticity of substitution between natural resources and other factors is high — significantly greater than unity — or resource-augmenting technological change has proceeded faster than overall productivity; (b) the elasticity of substitution between labor and capital is close to unity.

After these simulations were run, it appeared possible to estimate directly the parameters of the preferred form of production function. Econometric estimates confirm proposition (a) and seem to support the alternative of high elasticity of substitution between resources and the neoclassical factors.

Of course it is always possible that the future will be discontinuously different from the past. But if our estimates are accepted, then continuation of substitution during the next fifty years, during which many environmentalists foresee the end to growth, will result in a small increase — perhaps about 0.1 per cent per annum — in the growth of per capita income.

Is our economy, with its mixture of market processes and governmental controls, biased in favor of wasteful and shortsighted exploitation of natural resources? In considering this charge, two archetypical cases must be distinguished, although many actual cases fall between them. First, there are appropriable resources for which buyers pay market values and users market rentals. Second, there are inappropriable resources, "public goods," whose use appears free to individual producers and consumers but is costly in aggregate to society.

If the past is any guide for the future, there seems to be little reason to worry about the exhaustion of resources which the market already treats as economic goods. We have already commented on the irony that both growth men and antigrowth men invoke the interests of future generations. The issue between them is not whether and how much provision must be made for future generations, but in what form it should be made. The growth man emphasizes reproducible capital and education. The conservationist emphasizes exhaustible resources — minerals in the ground, open space, virgin land. The economist's initial presumption is that the market will decide in what forms to transmit wealth by the requirement that all kinds of wealth bear a comparable rate of return. Now stocks of natural resources — for example, mineral deposits — are essentially sterile. Their return to their owners is the increase in their prices relative to prices of other goods. In a properly functioning market economy, resources will be exploited at such a pace that their rate of relative price appreciation is competitive with rates of return on other kinds of capital. Many conservationists have noted such price appreciation with horror, but if the prices of these resources accurately reflect the scarcities of the future, they must rise in order to prevent too rapid exploitation. Natural resources *should* grow in relative scarcity — otherwise they are an inefficient way for society to hold and transmit wealth compared to productive physical and human capital. Price appreciation protects resources from premature exploitation.

How would an excessive rate of exploitation show up? We would see rates of relative price increase that are above the general real rate of return on wealth. This would indicate that society had in the past used precious resources too profligately, relative to the tastes and technologies later revealed. The scattered evidence we have indicates little excessive price rise. For some resources, indeed, prices seem to have risen more slowly than efficient use would indicate ex post.

If this reasoning is correct, the nightmare of a day of reckoning and economic collapse when, for example, all fossil fuels are forever gone seems to be based on failure to recognize the existing and future possibilities of substitute materials and processes. As the day of reckoning approaches, fuel prices will provide — as they do not now — strong incentives for such substitutions, as well as for the conservation of remaining supplies. On the other hand, the warnings of the conservationists and scientists do underscore the importance of continuous monitoring of the national and world outlook for energy and other resources. Substitutability might disappear. Conceivably both the market and public agencies might be too complacent about the prospects for new and safe substitutes for fossil fuels. The opportunity and need for fruitful collaboration between economists and physical scientists has never been greater.

Possible abuse of public natural resources is a much more serious problem. It is useful to distinguish between *local* and *global* ecological disturbances. The former include transient air pollution, water pollution, noise pollution, visual disamenities. It is certainly true that we have not charged automobile users and electricity consumers for their pollution of the skies, or farmers and housewives for the pollution of lakes by the runoff of fertilizers and detergents. In that degree our national product series have overestimated the advance of welfare. Our urban disamenity estimates given above indicate a current overestimate of about 5 per cent of total consumption.

There are other serious consequences of treating as free things which are not really free. This practice gives the wrong signals for the directions of economic growth. The producers of automobiles and of electricity should be given incentives to develop and to utilize "cleaner" technologies. The consumers of automobiles and electricity should pay in higher prices for the pollution they cause, or for the higher costs of low-pollution processes. If recognition of these costs causes consumers to shift their purchases to other goods and services, that is only efficient. At present overproduction of these goods is uneconomically subsidized as truly as if the producers received cash subsidies from the Treasury.

The mistake of the antigrowth men is to blame economic growth per se for the misdirection of economic growth. The misdirection is due to a defect of the pricing system — a serious but by no means irreparable defect and one which would in any case be present in a stationary economy. Pollutants have multiplied much faster than the population or the economy during the last thirty years. Although general economic growth has intensified the problem, it seems to originate in particular technologies. The proper remedy is to correct the price system so as to discourage these technologies. Zero economic growth is a blunt instrument for cleaner air, prodigiously expensive and probably ineffectual.

As for the danger of global ecological catastrophes, there is probably very little that economics alone can say. Maybe we are pouring pollutants into the atmosphere at such a rate that we will melt the polar icecaps and flood all the world's seaports. Unfortunately, there seems to be great uncertainty about the causes and the likelihood of such occurrences. These catastrophic global disturbances warrant a higher priority for research than the local disturbances to which so much attention has been given.

POPULATION GROWTH

Like the role of natural resources, the role of population in the standard neoclassical model is ripe for re-examination. The assumption is that population and labor force grow exogenously, like compound interest. Objections arise on both descriptive and normative grounds. We know that population growth cannot continue forever. Some day there will be stable or declining population, either with high birth and death rates and short life expectancies, or with low birth and death rates and long life expectancies. As Richard Easterlin argues in his National Bureau book,[4] there surely is some adaptation of human fertility and mortality to economic circumstances. Alas, neither economists nor other social scientists have been notably successful in developing a theory of fertility that corresponds even roughly to the facts. The subject deserves much more attention from economists and econometricians than it has received.

On the normative side, the complaint is that economists should not fatalistically acquiesce in whatever population growth happens. They should instead help to frame a population policy. Since the costs to society of additional children may exceed the costs to the parents, childbearing decisions are a signal example of market failure. How to internalize the full social costs of reproduction is an even more challenging problem than internalizing the social costs of pollution.

During the past ten years, the fertility of the United States population has declined dramatically. If continued, this trend would soon diminish fertility to a level ultimately consistent with zero population growth. But such trends have been reversed in the past, and in the absence of any real understanding of the determinants of fertility, predictions are extremely hazardous.

The decline may be illustrated by comparing the 1960 and 1967 net reproduction rates and intrinsic (economists would say "equilibrium") rates of growth of the United States population. The calculations of Table 3 refer to the asymptotic steady-state implications of indefinite continuation of the age-specific fertility and mortality rates of the year 1960 or 1967. Should the trend of the 1960s continue, the intrinsic growth rate would become zero, and the net reproduction rate 1.000, in the 1970s. Supposing that the decline in fertility then stopped. The actual population would grow slowly for another forty or fifty

---

[4] *Population, Labor Force, and Long Swings in Economic Growth: The American Experience,* New York, NBER, 1968.

TABLE 3
U.S. Population Characteristics in Equilibrium

	Intrinsic Growth Rate (per cent per year)	Net Reproduction Rate	Median Age
1960 fertility-mortality	2.1362	1.750	21–22
1967 fertility-mortality	0.7370	1.221	28
Hypothetical ZPG	0.0000	1.000	32

years while the inherited bulge in the age distribution at the more fertile years gradually disappeared. The asymptotic size of the population would be between 250 million and 300 million.

One consequence of slowing down the rate of population growth by diminished fertility is, of course, a substantial increase in the age of the equilibrium population, as indicated in the third column of Table 3. It is hard to judge to what degree qualitative change and innovation have in the past been dependent on quantitative growth. When our institutions are expanding in size and in number, deadwood can be gracefully bypassed and the young can guide the new. In a stationary population, institutional change will either be slower or more painful.

The current trend in fertility in the United States suggests that, contrary to the pessimistic warnings of some of the more extreme anti-growth men, it seems quite possible that ZPG can be reached while childbearing remains a voluntary private decision. Government policy can concentrate on making it completely voluntary by extending the availability of birth control knowledge and technique and of legal abortion. Since some 20 per cent of current births are estimated to be unintended, it may well be that intended births at present are insufficient to sustain the population.

Once the rate of population growth is regarded as a variable, perhaps one subject to conscious social control, the neoclassical growth model can tell some of the consequences of its variation. As explained above, sustainable per capita consumption (growing at the rate of technological progress) requires enough net investment to increase the capital stock at the natural rate of growth of the economy (the sum of the rate of increase of population and productivity). Given the capital-output ratio, sustainable consumption per capita will be larger the lower the rate of population increase; at the same time, the capital-widening requirement is diminished.

This is, however, not the only effect of a reduction of the rate of population growth. The equilibrium capital-output ratio itself is altered. The average wealth of a population is a weighted average of the wealth positions of people of different ages. Over its life cycle the typical family, starting from low or negative net worth, accumulates wealth to spend in old age, and perhaps in middle years when children are most costly. Now a stationary or slow-growing population has a characteristic age distribution much different from that of a rapidly growing population. The stationary population will have relatively fewer people in the early low-wealth years, but relatively more in the late low-wealth

TABLE 4

Illustrative Relationship of Sustainable Per Capita Consumption to Marginal Productivity of Capital and to Capital-Output Ratio

Marginal Productivity of Capital					Index of Consumption Per Capita (c)		
Gross (R)	Net of Depreciation ($R - \delta$)	Ratio of Capital to GNP (μ')	Ratio of Capital to NNP (μ)	Index of NNP per Capita (y)	1960 Pop. Growth	1967 Pop. Growth	ZPG
(1)	(2)	(3)	(4)	(5)	(6)	(7)	(8)
.09	.05	3.703	4.346	1.639	1.265	1.372	1.426
.105	.065	3.175	3.637	1.556	1.265	1.344	1.386
.12	.08	2.778	3.125	1.482	1.245	1.309	1.343
.15	.11	2.222	2.439	1.356	1.187	1.233	1.257

Note: A Cobb-Douglas production function is assumed for GNP, with constant returns to scale, with an elasticity of output with respect to capital (α) of $1/3$, and with the rate (γ) of labor-augmenting technological progress 3 per cent per year. The depreciation rate (δ) is assumed to be 4 per cent per year. GNP per capita (Y) is $ae^{\gamma t}k^\alpha$ and NNP per capita (y) is $Y - \delta k$, where k is the capital-labor ratio.

Column 3: Since $Rk = \alpha Y$, $\mu' = k/Y = \alpha/R$.

Column 4: $\mu = \mu'/(1 - \delta\mu')$.

Column 5: $y = (1 - \delta\mu')Y$. For the index, $ae^{\gamma t}$ is set equal to 1.

Columns 6, 7, and 8: $c = [1 - (n + \gamma)\mu]y$. Given $\gamma = 0.03$, $n + \gamma$ is 0.0513 for 1960, 0.0374 for 1967, 0.0300 for ZPG.

TABLE 5

Desired Wealth-Income Ratios Estimated for Different Rates of Population Growth (and for Different Equivalent Adult Scales and Subjective Discount Rates [a])

Net Interest Rate $(R - \delta)$	Desired Wealth-Income Ratio (μ)		
	1960 Pop. Growth (.021)	1967 Pop. Growth (.007)	ZPG
Teenagers, 1.0; Children, 1.0; Discount, 0.02			
.05	−1.70	−1.46	−1.24
.065	0.59	0.91	1.16
.08	2.31	2.70	2.90
.11	4.31	4.71	4.95
Teenagers, 0.8; Children, 0.6; Discount, 0.01			
.05	0.41	0.74	0.97
.065	2.36	2.75	3.00
.08	3.74	4.16	4.41
.11	5.17	5.55	5.75
Teenagers, 0.8; Children, 0.6; Discount, 0.02			
.05	−1.17	−0.95	−0.75
.065	1.08	1.38	1.60
.08	2.74	3.11	3.34
.11	4.61	4.98	5.18
Teenagers, 0.0; Children, 0.0; Discount, 0.02			
.05	−0.40	−0.15	0.02
.065	1.93	2.20	2.36
.08	3.56	3.85	4.01
.11	5.20	5.47	5.61

Note: The desired wealth-income ratio is calculated for a given steady state of population increase and the corresponding equilibrium age distribution. It is an aggregation of the wealth and income positions of households of different ages. As explained in Appendix C it also depends on the interest rate, the typical age-income profile and the expected growth of incomes ($\gamma = 0.03$), the rate of subjective discount of future utility of consumption, and the weights given to teenagers (boys 14–20 and girls 14–18) and other children in household allocations of lifetime incomes to consumption in different years. See Appendix C for further explanation.

[a] Shown in boldface.

TABLE 6
Estimated Equilibrium Capital-Output Ratios
and Per Capita Consumption Rates [a]

Population Growth Rate	Interest Rate $(R - \delta)$	Capital-Output Ratio (μ)	Consumption Index (c)	Per Cent Increase in c over 1960
Teenagers, 1.0; Children, 1.0; Discount, 0.02				
1960	.089	2.88	1.23	
1967	.085	2.99	1.30	5.62
ZPG	.082	3.07	1.34	9.04
Teenagers, 0.8; Children, 0.6; Discount, 0.01				
1960	.074	3.28	1.25	
1967	.071	3.38	1.33	6.23
ZPG	.069	3.47	1.37	9.74
Teenagers, 0.8; Children, 0.6; Discount, 0.02				
1960	.084	3.00	1.24	
1967	.080	3.11	1.31	5.82
ZPG	.078	3.16	1.35	8.97
Teenagers, 0.0; Children, 0.0; Discount, 0.02				
1960	.077	3.22	1.25	
1967	.074	3.28	1.32	6.42
ZPG	.073	3.33	1.36	9.99

Note: Estimated by interpolation from Tables 4 and 5. See Figure 1.
[a] Equivalent adult scales and subjective discount rate are shown in boldface.

years. So it is not obvious in which direction the shift of weights moves the average.

We have, however, estimated the shift by a series of calculations described in Appendix C. Illustrative results are shown in Tables 4–6 and Figure 1. Evidently, reduction in the rate of growth increases the society's desired wealth-income ratio. This means an increase in the capital-output ratio which increases the society's sustainable consumption per capita.[5]

On both counts, therefore, a reduction in population increase

---

[5] Provided only that the change is made from an initial situation in which the net marginal productivity of capital exceeds the economy's natural rate of growth. Otherwise the increased capital-widening requirements exceed the gains in output.

FIGURE 1

Determination of Equilibrium Capital-Output Ratio and Interest Rate
(*equivalent adult scale for teenagers and children* = 1.0; *subjective discount rate* = 0.02)

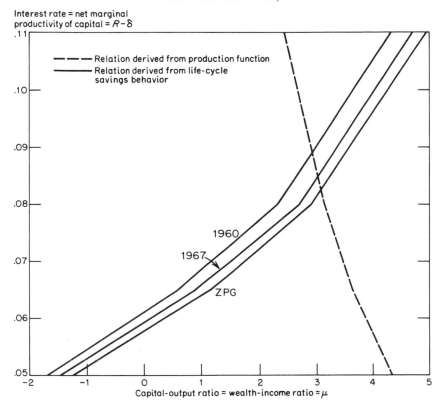

Interest rate = net marginal
productivity of capital = $R - \delta$

- – – – Relation derived from production function
- —— Relation derived from life-cycle savings behavior

1960

1967

ZPG

Capital-output ratio = wealth-income ratio = μ

Source: Tables 4 and 5.

should raise sustainable consumption. We have essayed an estimate of the magnitude of this gain. In a ZPG equilibrium sustainable consumption per capita would be 9–10 per cent higher than in a steady state of 2.1 per cent growth corresponding to 1960 fertility and mortality, and somewhat more than 3 per cent higher than in a steady state of 0.7 per cent growth corresponding to 1967 fertility and mortality.

These neoclassical calculations do not take account of the lower pressure of population growth on natural resources. As between the 1960 equilibrium and ZPG, the diminished drag of resource limitations is worth about one-tenth of 1 per cent per annum in growth of per capita consumption. Moreover, if our optimistic estimates of the ease of substitution of other factors of production for natural resources are wrong, a slowdown of population growth will have much more important effects in postponing the day of reckoning.

Is growth obsolete? We think not. Although GNP and other national income aggregates are imperfect measures of welfare, the broad picture of secular progress which they convey remains after correction of their most obvious deficiencies. At present there is no reason to arrest general economic growth to conserve natural resources, although there is good reason to provide proper economic incentives to conserve resources which currently cost their users less than true social cost. Population growth cannot continue indefinitely, and evidently it is already slowing down in the United States. This slowdown will significantly increase sustainable per capita consumption. But even with ZPG there is no reason to shut off technological progress. The classical stationary state need not become our utopian norm.

APPENDIX A: A MEASURE OF ECONOMIC WELFARE

The purpose of this appendix is to explain the "measure of economic welfare" (MEW) introduced in the text. Conceptually it is a comprehensive measure of the annual real consumption of households. Consumption is intended to include all goods and services, marketed or not, valued at market prices or at their equivalent in opportunity costs to consumers. Collective public consumption is to be included, whether provided by government or otherwise; and allowance is to be made for negative externalities, such as those due to environmental damage and to the disamenities and congestion of urbanization and industrialization. Real consumption is estimated by valuing the flows of goods and services at constant prices.

We distinguish sustainable welfare (MEW-S) from actual welfare (MEW-A). Sustainable MEW is the amount of consumption in any year that is consistent with sustained steady growth in per capita consumption at the trend rate of technological progress. MEW, whether sustainable or actual, can be expressed either in aggregate or in per capita terms. For obvious reasons set forth in the text, we regard the per capita measure as the more relevant one, a judgment that enters into the very definition of MEW-S.

Actual MEW excludes all final output actually devoted to capital replacement and accumulation. Sustainable MEW excludes the capital expenditures needed to sustain the capital-output ratio. It allows for capital depreciation, for equipping new members of the labor force, and for increasing capital per worker at the trend rate of productivity change. MEW-S will be greater than MEW-A in years when the economy is investing more than these requirements, and smaller when it is investing less. In a neoclassical growth model, an excess of MEW-S over MEW-A means that the capital-output ratio is rising, the economy is moving to a higher equilibrium growth path, and MEW-S is increasing faster than the trend rate of technological progress. An excess of MEW-A over MEW-S means the opposite.

We have not attempted to estimate a concept of "potential MEW" —analogous to potential GNP—which would correct for fluctuations in utilization of the labor force and the capital stock. Consequently comparisons of MEW, actual or sustainable, are best confined to periods of comparable utilization. The end points of our trial calculations, 1929 and 1965, are roughly comparable in this respect.

We are aiming for a consumption measure, but we cannot of course estimate how well individual and collective happiness are correlated with consumption. We cannot say whether a modern society with cars, airplanes, and television sets is really happier than the nation of our great-grandparents who lived without use or knowledge of these inventions. We cannot estimate the externalities of social interdependence, of which Veblen, Galbraith, and other social critics have complained. That is, we cannot tell to what degree increases in consumption are offset by displeasure that others are also increasing their consumption. Nor can we tell how much consumption is simply the relief of artificially induced cravings nurtured by advertising and sales effort.

In suggesting a consumption-oriented measure, we do not in any way derogate the importance of the conventional national income accounts. They are, of course, the chief and indispensable source of our calculations, which are for the most part simply a rearrangement of the data the Department of Commerce faithfully and skillfully provides. Gross national product and net national product are measures of output performance. As such, they are the relevant measures both for short-run stabilization policy and for assessing the economy's long-run progress as a productive machine.

Our purpose is different and suggests a different measure. Consider, for example, the treatment of defense expenditure, which rose from less than 1 per cent of GNP in 1929 to 10 per cent in 1965. The capacity of the economy to meet this rise in defense demands, along with others, certainly deserves to be counted in assessing its gains in productive performance between the two dates. But we exclude defense expenditures because they add to neither actual nor sustainable household consumption. This exclusion does not charge the rise in defense expenditures as an inevitable by-product of the growth of the economy, nor does it imply any judgment as to their necessity or desirability. It simply acknowledges that this component of GNP growth, whatever its causes and consequences, does not enter via normal economic processes into the consumption satisfactions of households.

We recognize that our proposal is controversial on conceptual and theoretical grounds and that many of the numerical expedients in its execution are dubious. Nevertheless, the challenge to economists to produce relevant welfare-oriented measures seems compelling enough to justify some risk-taking. We hope that others will be challenged, or provoked, to tackle the problem with different assumptions, more refined procedures, and better data. We hope also that further investigations will be concerned with the distribution, as well as the mean value, of a measure of economic welfare, an aspect we have not been able to consider.

In the remaining sections of this appendix we explain the details of the calculations presented in text Table 1. Section A.1 concerns reclassification of expenditures reported in national income accounts to obtain a more comprehensive concept of consumption. This reclassification implies some adjustments in the capital accounts presented in section A.2. In section A.3 we describe our imputations for consumption yielded by nonmarket activities; and in section A.4, our adjustments for the disamenities of urban growth. Section A.5 describes the final estimates, and section A.6 contains some discussion of their reliability.

A.1 Reclassification of Final Expenditures

A.1.1 Government Purchases.   In the United States income and product accounts, government purchases of goods and services are counted as final output and are not classified as consumption and investment. For our purposes, we need to classify government uses of resources as (a) consumption, (b) replacement and accumulation of capital contributing to future consumption possibilities, (c) "regrettable" outlays that use resources for national purposes other than consumption or capital formation supportive of future consumption, and

TABLE A.1
Reclassification of Government Purchases of Goods and Services, Various Years, 1929–65
(*billions of dollars, 1958 prices*)

		1929	1935	1945	1947	1954	1958	1965
1	Public consumption	0.3	0.3	0.4	0.5	0.5	0.8	1.2
2	Public investment, gross	15.0	19.3	9.7	18.6	30.6	37.0	50.3
3	Regrettables	1.7	2.0	139.7	14.4	49.4	46.4	47.6
4	Intermediate goods and services	5.0	5.4	6.6	6.4	8.4	10.0	15.6
5	Total government consumption and investment	15.3	19.6	10.1	19.1	31.1	37.8	51.5
6	Total government purchases	22.0	27.0	156.4	39.9	88.9	94.2	114.7

Note: For 1954–65, based on current-dollar figures for federal and state and local purchases of goods and services, NIP Table 3.10 (see note 6, above), deflated by government purchases deflator, NIP Table 8.1. Line 6 is also line 20 of NIP Table 1.2.

Consumption: postal service (line 52) and recreation (line 61).

Investment: one-half atomic energy development (line 4), education (line 16), health and hospitals (line 21), commerce, transportation, and housing (line 39), conservation and development of resources (line 60), and agriculture (line 54).

Regrettables: national defense (line 2) less one-half atomic energy development (line 4), space research and technology (line 6), international affairs and finance (line 13), and veterans benefits and services (line 33).

Intermediate: everything else, including general government (line 7), sanitation (line 22), and civilian safety (line 28).

For 1929–47, NIP Table 3.10 is not available, and the breakdowns were based on estimates by broad expenditure category.

(d) provision of intermediate goods and services instrumental to final production. The results of our classifications are shown in Table A.1.

Very little government expenditure on goods and services can be considered consumption. From the functional breakdown in the national accounts, we take as consumption only the subsidy of the post office and recreation outlays (NIP Table 3.10).[6]

We have counted as gross investment only items that raise productivity (education, medicine, public health) or yield services directly consumed by households (housing, transportation). Investment so defined represents 65 per cent of government purchases in 1929 and 43

[6] References to NIP tables are to the standard tables of the Department of Commerce, *National Income and Product Accounts of the United States, 1929–1965* and to the annual extensions or revisions of these data in July issues of the *Survey of Current Business*.

per cent in 1965. It is, of course, necessary to account for the yield of government capital investments. In some cases the yield consists of increased factor incomes and is automatically registered. In other cases imputations for the consumption of the services of government capital are necessary. This is discussed in section A.2, below.

"Regrettables" represent final expenditures — made for reasons of national security, prestige, or diplomacy — which in our judgment do not directly increase the economic welfare of households. We will discuss further the most important case, national defense; the reasoning is similar for other regrettables.

Defense expenditures have no direct value in household consumption. No reasonable nation purchases defense because its services are desired per se. The product of defense outlays is national security, but it is clearly not true that our security has increased as the outlays rose a hundredfold from 1929 to 1965. Changes in international relations and in military technology have vastly multiplied the costs of providing a given level of security. Just as we count the fruits of scientific progress, managerial improvement, and mineral discovery when they make it easier for the nation to wrest its living from the environment, so we must count the results of deterioration in the nation's economic or political environment. This procedure does not blame the economy for unfavorable international political events any more than recording a reduction in food crops due to bad weather or a plague of locusts means that the agricultural economy has become any less efficient.

The final category, "intermediate goods and services," is clearest when the government is providing direct services or materials to business enterprises. It also includes more diffuse instrumental outlays: the costs of maintaining a sanitary and safe natural and social environment. There is no sharp dividing line between intermediate overhead expenditures and regrettables. Police protection, for example, might fall under either category.

A.1.2 Private Purchases.   We have also made some reclassifications of private expenditures: (a) Personal business expenses and one-fifth of personal transportation expenses (an estimate of the fraction devoted to commutation) are subtracted from consumption and regarded as intermediate or instrumental (Table A.16, line 2). (b) Educational and medical outlays are regarded as gross investments (Table A.16, line 4). (c) All outlays for consumer durables, not just purchases of residences, are treated as investments (Table A.16, line 3). (d) Imputations are made for those services of consumer capital that are directly consumed (Table A.16, line 5); these are described in section A.2.

A.2   Adjustments for Capital

Conventional national income accounting limits investment to domestic business investment and residential construction. Economists have come to include a much wider group of expenditures in this category. Table A.2 gives a list of the conventional items and those added for our present purposes, for the year 1958.

The three important accounting problems introduced by this treatment of capital are (a) calculation of the net stock of wealth; (b) calculation of imputed services from capital to be added to consumption; (c) decomposition of gross investment into capital consumption and net investment to calculate sustainable MEW.

A.2.1   Net Stock of Wealth.   Most of the figures for components of wealth have been gathered from other sources. They are shown in Table A.3. The figures for educational capital and health capital have

TABLE A.2
Items of Gross Investment, 1958
(dollars in billions)

	Investment	Per Cent of Total
Conventional items		
1. Business investment	$ 40.1	25.4%
2. Residential construction	20.8	13.2
New items		
3. Government investment	37.0	23.5
4. Consumer durables	37.9	24.0
5. Other consumer investments	19.6	12.4
6. Net foreign investment	2.2	1.4
Total	$157.6	100.0%

Source (for NIP, see note 6, above):

Line
1   NIP Table 1.2, lines 8–14
2   NIP Table 1.2, line 11
3   Table A.1, line 2
4   NIP Table 1.2, line 3
5   NIP Table 2.5, lines 42 plus 93 less 44
6   NIP Table 1.2, line 6

TABLE A.3
Net Stock of Public and Private Wealth, Various Years, 1929–65
(billions of dollars, 1958 prices)

	1929	1935	1945	1947	1954	1958	1965
1 Net reproducible capital	765.6	742.3	832.5	895.3	1,186.6	1,367.6	1,676.2
2 Nonreproducible capital *a*	299.0	276.1	245.9	262.2	299.9	335.4	392.4
3 Educational capital	91.2	120.2	253.2	269.0	447.2	581.6	879.4
4 Health	7.2	28.7	44.5	49.5	74.8	89.5	121.2
5 Total	1,163.0	1,167.3	1,376.1	1,476.0	2,008.5	2,374.1	3,069.2

Source: Lines 1 and 2: 1929–58 from Raymond W. Goldsmith, *The National Wealth of the United States in the Postwar Period,* Princeton for NBER, 1962, Tables A-1, A-2, and A-16; 1965, from John Kendrick's estimates presented in *Statistical Abstract of the United States,* 1967, Tables 492 and 494. Figures for 1935 and 1965 are linear interpolations.

Line 3: See text.

Line 4: Deflated health expenditures, public and private, cumulated on the assumption of an exponential depreciation rate of 20 per cent per annum. Public health expenditures are given in NIP Table 3.10, line 21; private expenditures, NIP Table 2.5, line 42 (see note 6, above).

a Nonreproducible capital covers five categories, which are listed below with their relative importance in 1958:

	Share of Total Value of Nonreproducible Assets, 1958 (per cent)
Agricultural land	30.2
Residential land	18.1
Nonresidential land	32.2
Public land	12.2
Net foreign assets	7.3
Total	100.0

been constructed in part by us. The estimates of tangible capital, reproducible and nonreproducible, are from Goldsmith and Kendrick.[7]

The data on nonreproducible wealth are dubious. In principle, the increased value in constant prices of nonreproducible assets comes primarily through upgrading land from agricultural to nonagricultural

[7] Raymond W. Goldsmith, *The National Wealth of the United States in the Postwar Period,* Princeton for NBER, 1962; and John W. Kendrick, *Productivity Trends in the United States,* Princeton for NBER, 1961.

uses.[8] In practice, given the nature of the estimates, some of the recorded increase may be due to improper deflation.

The value of educational capital is based on Schultz's estimates of the cost per pupil of attained education, valued at 1956 costs of each level of education. This assumes no technological change in education. We preferred to treat education in a similar way to other forms of wealth and to value it at replacement cost at constant prices rather than at constant 1956 costs. We therefore used Machlup's series of average cost per pupil to get an index of cost per pupil in constant prices. We then recalculated Schultz's figures to obtain the value of educational capital per member of the labor force.[9]

The value of health capital was constructed by cumulating deflated public and private medical health and hospital expenditures. These were cumulated assuming exponential depreciation at 20 per cent per annum.

A.2.2 Services from Wealth.   Having shifted some public and private expenditures from consumption to investment, we must impute consumption of services of those types of capital whose yield does not take the form of explicit factor earnings. Such imputations are made in the national accounts only for owner-occupied housing.

For both consumer durable expenditures and government structures (excluding military), Juster has prepared estimates of capital services.[10] We have used his estimates for services, and these are presented in Table A.4. It should be noted that this imputation is not entirely appropriate, since some of the imputed output is intermediate (that is, used by business). On the other hand, his assumed rates of return seem quite low, and this low estimate may offset the erroneous inclusion of some intermediate product.

We do not impute any consumption services to health or educational capital. To the extent that health and education expenditures lead to higher productivity, there is no need for further imputation. We make the admittedly extreme assumption that no direct gains in satisfaction are produced by these categories of wealth. Since they have

---

[8] See Goldsmith, *National Wealth*, p. 48, n. 2.

[9] Data are from Theodore Schultz, "Education and Economic Growth," in N. B. Henry, ed., *Social Forces Influencing American Education*, Chicago, University of Chicago Press, 1961; Fritz Machlup, *The Production and Distribution of Knowledge in the United States*, Princeton, Princeton University Press, 1962.

[10] F. Thomas Juster, *Household Capital Formation and Its Financing, 1897–1962*, New York, NBER, 1966, App. B.

TABLE A.4

Imputed Services from Consumer Durables and Civilian Government
Structures, Various Years, 1929–65

(*billions of dollars*)

	1929	1935	1945	1947	1954	1958	1965
				Current Prices			
Imputed net rental							
Consumer	3.6	1.9	3.5	5.6	10.6	13.9	23.2
Government	0.4	0.5	1.8	2.8	3.8	5.0	6.3
Capital consumption							
Consumer	6.2	4.2	7.9	12.2	21.7	26.9	44.9
Government	1.5	1.7	2.8	3.9	6.4	9.0	11.8
Total services	11.7	8.3	16.0	24.5	42.5	54.8	86.2
				1958 Prices			
Consumer services	24.9	17.8	22.1	26.7	37.2	40.8	62.3
Government services	4.8	6.4	8.9	10.0	11.7	14.0	16.6
Total services	29.7	24.2	31.1	36.7	49.0	54.8	78.9

Source: Figures in current prices are from F. Thomas Juster, *Household Capital Formation and Its Financing, 1897–1962,* New York, NBER, 1966, Tables B-2 and B-4. The constant-price series is obtained by dividing by the deflator for fixed investment.

The figures for 1965 were extrapolated from 1962 using data on purchases and depreciation of consumer durables.

been growing faster than the other stocks, our assumption may lead to understatement of the growth of welfare.

A.2.3 Capital Consumption and Net Investment. In Table A.5 we show first, in lines 1, 6, and 7, the national accounts figures for gross investment, capital consumption, and net investment. For our MEW we have, as explained above, broadened the concepts of capital and investment. Lines 5, 8, and 9 give estimates for the MEW concepts of gross investment, capital consumption, and change in capital stock. Capital consumption, line 8, is estimated from the wealth data of Table A.3 above.

In addition, we have estimated a new concept of net investment, called net MEW investment. This is the amount of investment to be added to actual MEW to obtain sustainable MEW. Zero net MEW investment corresponds to that gross investment which would keep per capita consumption growing at the rate of technological progress. In

TABLE A.5
Gross and Net Investment in National Accounts (NIPA) and in Measure of Economic Welfare (MEW), Various Years, 1929–65

	1929	1935	1945	1947	1954	1958	1965
1. Gross investment, NIPA	40.4	18.0	19.6	51.5	59.4	60.9	99.2
2. Government purchases re-classified as investment for MEW	15.0	19.3	9.7	18.6	30.6	37.0	50.3
3. Consumer purchases reclassi-fied as investment for MEW							
a. Consumer durables	16.7	11.5	12.3	26.2	35.5	37.9	60.9
b. Education and health	6.5	6.3	9.1	10.4	15.3	19.6	30.1
4. Net foreign investment, NIPA and MEW	1.5	−1.0	−3.8	12.3	3.0	2.2	6.2
5. Gross investment, MEW	80.1	54.1	46.9	119.0	143.8	157.6	246.7
6. Capital consumption, NIPA	20.0	20.0	21.9	18.3	32.5	38.9	54.7
7. Net investment, NIPA	20.4	−2.0	−2.3	33.2	26.9	22.0	44.5
8. Capital consumption, MEW	39.3	53.4	33.6	69.1	67.7	66.2	147.4
9. Change in capital stock, MEW	40.8	0.7	13.3	49.9	76.1	91.4	99.3
10. Growth requirement, MEW	46.1	46.7	65.8	−5.4	63.1	78.9	101.8
11. Net investment, MEW	−5.3	−46.0	−52.5	55.3	13.0	12.5	−2.5

Source (for NIP, see note 6, above):

Line
1   NIP Table 1.2, line 6
2   Table A.1, line 2
3a NIP Table 1.1, line 3, deflated by the consumption deflator
3b NIP Table 2.5, lines 42 plus 93 less 44, all deflated by consumption deflator, NIP Table 8.1, line 2
4   NIP Table 1.2, line 17
5   Sum of lines 1–4
6   NIP Table 1.9, line 2, deflated by fixed investment deflator, NIP Table 8.1, line 7
7   Line 1 minus line 6
8   Line 5 minus line 9
9   Estimated on per annum basis from Table A.3
10 Annual increase in capital stock necessary to keep up with trend growth of labor forces and productivity. See text.
11 Line 8 minus line 10, or line 5 minus sum of lines 9 and 10

the standard neoclassical growth model, with labor-augmenting technical progress and a constant rate of labor force participation, this is also the gross investment necessary to maintain a constant ratio of capital to the effective or augmented labor force and a constant ratio of capital to output. The conventional net investment needed for this purpose we call the growth requirement (Table A.5, line 10). Net MEW investment (line 11) is change in capital stock less the growth requirement.

If NNP is a desirable measure of social income in a stationary economy, sustainable MEW is a natural analogue for a growing economy.[11] Indeed, in the special case of zero population growth and no technological change, sustainable MEW and NNP are identical. NNP, it will be recalled, is the amount of consumption that leaves the capital stock "intact." The reason for keeping *capital* intact in a stationary economy is that the same amount of consumption, in aggregate and per capita, will be available in future years. The reason for keeping the *capital-output ratio* intact in a growing economy is that per capita consumption will grow at the rate of technological progress.

An alternative concept of social income would be sustainable per capita consumption, which will be larger than sustainable MEW when there is technological progress. Per capita consumption can be sustained by technological advance even while the capital-output and capital-labor ratios steadily decline. With a production function that allows factor substitution, today's consumption standard could eventually be produced with a capital-labor ratio asymptotically approaching zero. During this process the marginal productivity of capital would steadily rise. Our proposed measure of social income is more austere and, we believe, more consonant with revealed social preference. We do not observe current generations consuming capital on the grounds that their successors will reap the benefits of technological progress.

A guiding principle for a definition of social income is the following: The social income is that amount of consumption that is consistent with the social valuation of investment at its current opportunity cost in terms of consumption. The social value of giving up an extra dollar of current consumption in favor of capital accumulation is the sum of the resulting increments to future consumption, each discounted by the appropriate social discount rate. When this value exceeds a dollar, investment is less than optimal and consumption should be reduced until

[11] See P. A. Samuelson, "The Evaluation of 'Social Income,'" in F. A. Lutz and D. C. Hague, eds., *The Theory of Capital,* London, Macmillan, 1961.

lowered capital yield and increased social discount rates combine to lower the value of investment to par. Similarly, when the stream of returns from a marginal dollar of investment sums to less than a dollar, current investment is too large and consumption too small. The amount of current consumption at which the marginal social value of investing a dollar at the expense of consumption is precisely a dollar may be regarded as the social income. It follows that the optimal amount of MEW net investment — defined as social income less actual consumption — is zero.

How do sustainable MEW and NNP relate to this principle? Under what conditions will these be the definitions of social income that follow from the valuation principle given above? Sufficient conditions can be presented formally. Let $c(t)$ be consumption per worker at time t and $L(t)$ the size of the work force. We assume that the labor force is a fixed proportion of the population; therefore, $c(t)$ can also be regarded as an index of per capita consumption. The labor force L is growing exponentially at rate n. Labor-augmenting technical progress is occurring at rate γ; so $L(t)e^{\gamma t}$ is the effective labor force, which is growing at rate $g = n + \gamma$. Gross output per worker is $e^{\gamma t}f(k)$, where k is the ratio of capital stock to effective labor force $K/Le^{\gamma t}$ and k' is the rate of change of k. Capital depreciates at the exponential rate δ.

The equation relating consumption, output, capital, and investment at every moment of time is:

$$c(t) = e^{\gamma(t)}\{f[k(t)] - (g + \delta)k(t) - k'(t)\}. \qquad \text{(A.1)}$$

Consider a feasible and efficient consumption plan: a sequence $c(t)$ for $t \geq 0$, feasible in the sense that it is consistent with (A.1), given the initial capital stock, $k(0)$, efficient in the sense that it would not be possible to increase any $c(t)$ without diminishing some other $c(t)$. We can then ask: What is the increase in per capita consumption at time θ that can be obtained by a unit reduction of per capita consumption at time 0 — the present — keeping the rest of the plan unchanged?

Let $r(t) = f'[k(t)] - \delta$, the net marginal productivity of capital at time t. Since the population is growing exponentially at rate n, the rates that transform per capita saving and investment today into per capita consumption in the future are $r(t) - n$; that is, a unit reduction of the rate of per capita consumption at time 0 will yield an increase of per capita consumption at time θ of

$$\exp\left\{\int_0^\theta [r(t) - n]dt\right\}$$

if consumption rates at all other times before and after θ are un-changed.[12]

If the consumption plan corresponds to a neoclassical growth equilibrium, k and r are constants and per capita consumption is growing at rate γ. The marginal trade-off of later for earlier consumption is $e^{(r-n)\theta}$ and depends only on the intervening time θ.

We turn now to the other half of the story, the social valuation of increments of future consumption yielded by current saving. Suppose that society's intertemporal preferences, at any current date designated by 0, can be described by a social welfare function,

$$U = \int_0^\infty u[c(t)]e^{-\rho t}dt,$$

where u is the one-period utility of consumption, and ρ is the constant pure rate of time preference at which utility is discounted. Let the one-period utility function be of the form $A + Bc^{1-\alpha}$ so that marginal utility $u'(c) = (1 - \alpha)Bc^{-\alpha}$, where α and $(1 - \alpha)B$ are positive. Furthermore, the elasticity of marginal utility with respect to consumption is $u''c/u' = -\alpha$. Holding U constant, the marginal rate of substitution between per capita consumption rates at θ and 0 is

$$\frac{u'[c(0)]}{u'[c(\theta)]} = \left[\frac{c(0)}{c(\theta)}\right]^{-\alpha}e^{\rho\theta}.$$

Thus the slope of any indifference curve between $c(\theta)$ and $c(0)$ is $-e^{-\rho\theta}$ along the 45° ray and $-e^{(\rho+\alpha\gamma)\theta}$ along the ray $c(\theta) = c(0)e^{\gamma\theta}$ (see Figure A.1).

---

[12] The rate at which incremental saving at time t can increase k, the ratio of capital to effective labor, is $r(t) - g$. Over the interval $(0, \theta)$ continuous reinvestment of the proceeds of incremental saving at time 0 will compound the increase in k to

$$\exp\left\{\int_0^\theta [r(t) - g]dt\right\}.$$

The increase of the aggregate capital stock will then be

$$L(0)e^{g\theta} \cdot \exp\left\{\int_0^\theta [r(t) - g]dt\right\} = L(0) \exp\left[\int_0^\theta r(t)dt\right].$$

This increment can be consumed during a small interval following time θ while leaving subsequent values of $k(t)$ at their original values, so that the initial consumption plan can be executed thereafter. Divided among the population $L(0)e^{n\theta}$ this gives an increment of per capita consumption of

$$\exp\left\{\int_0^\theta [r(t) - n]dt\right\}.$$

FIGURE A.1
Illustration of Balanced Growth as Optimal Consumption Plan
(ρ = *pure rate of social time preference*; α = *—elasticity of marginal
utility*; γ = *rate of technological progress*)

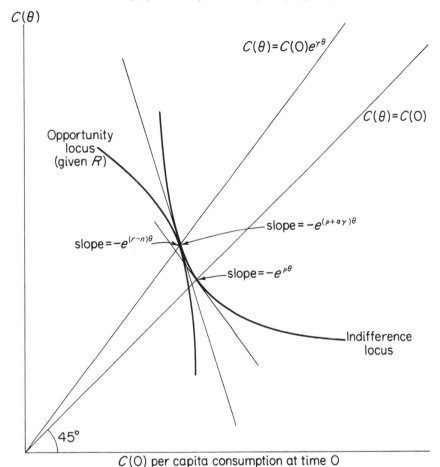

$C(\theta)$

$C(\theta)=C(0)e^{\gamma\theta}$

$C(\theta)=C(0)$

Opportunity
locus
(given R)

slope $=-e^{(\rho+\alpha\gamma)\theta}$

slope $=-e^{(r-n)\theta}$

slope $=-e^{\rho\theta}$

Indifference
locus

$45°$

$C(0)$ per capita consumption at time O

Under these assumptions the basic condition that must be met in
order that the social valuation of investment equal its cost in current
consumption is equality of the two intertemporal substitution rates, the
one reflecting production possibilities and the other social preferences.
They must be equal for every time interval θ:

$$\left[\frac{c(0)}{c(\theta)}\right]^{-\alpha} e^{\rho\theta} = \exp\left\{\int_0^\theta [r(t)-n]dt\right\}.$$

For a consumption path in equilibrium growth at rate γ, the condition reduces to $e^{(\rho+\alpha\gamma)\theta} = e^{(r-n)\theta}$. This will be true for all θ provided that $\rho + \alpha\gamma = r - n$.

If this condition is met, as illustrated in Figure A.1, the path of sustainable MEW—per capita consumption growing at rate γ—fulfills the basic principle for definition of social income.[13]

In the absence of technological progress and population growth, the condition is simply $\rho = r$. The path of NNP—constant per capita and aggregate consumption—meets the condition that the net marginal productivity of capital equal the pure social rate of time preference.

To summarize, social income is the amount society can consume without shortchanging the future. Thus social income refers to a consumption path along which saving and investment are, according to social valuations of their future yields, just worth their cost in current consumption. Under special conditions this path may be one with per capita consumption growing steadily at the rate of technological progress, and sustainable MEW is then the appropriate measure of social income. In our economy revealed social preference seems to support our inference that the consumption plan is one of ever-growing consumption per capita and our use of social valuations that are consistent with steady growth.

A.3 Imputation for Nonmarket Activities: Time Components of Consumption

Only a fraction of a lifetime is spent in gainful employment, but it is that fraction alone that shows up in output and consumption as ordinarily measured. Leisure and nonmarket work grow steadily in importance, and their omission can bias downward estimates of trends

---

[13] The result can also be derived by explicitly maximizing U with respect to $k'(t)$, given $k(0)$, using (A.1). The first-order conditions are:

$$\int_t^\infty u'[c(v)]e^{\gamma v}\{f'[k(v)] - (g + \delta)\}e^{-\rho(v-t)}dv = e^{\gamma t}u'[c(t)] \text{ for all } t \geq 0.$$

Differentiating this with respect to t gives

$$-u'[c(t)]e^{\gamma t}[r(t) - g]e^{-\rho t} = (\gamma - \rho)e^{(\gamma-\rho)t}u'[c(t)] + e^{(\gamma-\rho)t}u''[c(t)]c'(t).$$

Using $-\alpha = u''c/u'$ we have the general requirement that

$$r(t) - g = \rho - \gamma + \alpha \frac{c'(t)}{c(t)}.$$

An equilibrium growth path will meet this condition if and only if the constant value of k that characterizes it produces a value of r such that $r - n = \rho + \alpha\gamma$.

of per capita consumption. Imputation of the consumption value of leisure and nonmarket work presents severe conceptual and statistical problems. Since the magnitudes are large, differences in resolution of these problems make big differences in overall MEW estimates.

A.3.1 Conceptual Issues.   Consider an individual dividing a fixed endowment of time R among gainful employment W, leisure L, and nonmarket productive activity H. From the earnings of his employment he purchases consumption C. Let v_t be the real wage; $v_t p_t^C$, the money wage; and p_t^C, the price of market consumption goods, all for year t. These prices can be observed. Let p_t^L be the price of an hour of the consumption good leisure, and p_t^H the price of an hour's worth of the consumption good produced by home activity. These prices cannot be observed, and this is the source of the problem. Take all base-period prices, v_0, p_0, p_0^C, p_0^L, p_0^H, to be 1.

On the principle that the individual can on the margin exchange leisure or nonmarket activity for market consumption at the money wage $v_t p_t^C$, we can estimate the total money value of his consumption as $v_t p_t^C W_t + v_t p_t^C H_t + v_t p_t^C L_t$. But what did he get for his "money"? The three components of consumption must be "deflated" by the relevant prices p_t^C, p_t^H, p_t^L. This gives an expression for real consumption

$$v_t W_t + \frac{v_t p_t^C}{p_t^H} H_t + \frac{v_t p_t^C}{p_t^L} L_t.$$

Since real consumption at time zero is by definition R, the consumption index is:

$$v_t \frac{W_t}{R} + \frac{v_t p_t^C}{p_t^H} \frac{H_t}{R} + \frac{v_t p_t^C}{p_t^L} \frac{L_t}{R}. \tag{A.2}$$

The basic issue is whether the consumption prices of nonmarket uses of time have (a) risen with wage rates, or (b) risen with the prices of market consumption goods. On the first assumption, an hour not sold on the market is still an hour, the same in 1965 as in 1929. The only gains in consumption that can be credited on this account are the reductions in hours of work. On the second assumption, an hour not sold in the market has increased in consumption value the same as an hour worked, namely, by the increase in the real wage.

In our numerical estimates below we have calculated three variants:

Variant A: $p_t^H = p_t^L = v_t p_t^C$. The index (A.2) is then $1 + (v_t - 1)(W_t/R)$.
Variant B: $p_t^H = p_t^C$; $p_t^L = v_t p_t^C$. The index is $1 + (v_t - 1)[(W_t + H_t)/R]$.
Variant C: $p_t^H = p_t^L = p_t^C$. The index is $1 + (v_t - 1) = v_t$.

Variant A is the most conservative alternative. (C) is the most optimistic alternative.

The essential question is whether nonmarket activities have shared in the technical progress that has raised real wages. If this progress has been time-augmenting, not simply work-augmenting, then the optimistic alternative is correct. But if technology has increased solely the effectiveness of on-the-job work, the pessimistic alternative is correct.

The alternatives can be shown diagrammatically if we confine ourselves to two instead of three uses of time. In Figure A.2, the horizon-

FIGURE A.2

Alternative Interpretations of Welfare Gains Accompanying Wage Increases

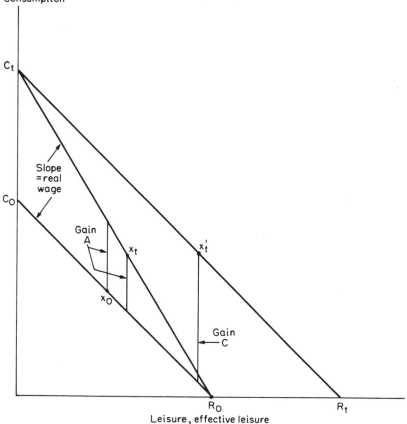

tal axis measures leisure; and the vertical axis, market consumption. The line R_0C_0 represents the opportunity locus in the base period; its slope is -1, on the convention that the base-period real wage is scaled at unity. The point x_0 represents the individual's choice. In period t the real wage has increased to v_t, the slope of the new opportunity locus is R_0C_t, and the selected point is x_t. According to the pessimistic interpretation, the gain in welfare, measured in market consumption, is approximated by the vertical difference between the two lines R_0C_0 and R_0C_t, measured either up from x_0 or down from x_t. The individual's time has not increased, and he gains from the higher real wage only in the degree that he works.

The optimistic interpretation is that technological progress has augmented his time, so that in terms of *effective* leisure and consumption the opportunity locus has shifted outward to R_tC_t. The real wage per effective hour is unchanged, although it has increased in terms of natural hours. The point x_t is, in terms of effective leisure, really x_t'. The increment in welfare is approximated by the vertical difference between the parallel lines R_0C_0 and R_tC_t, and is independent of the amount of time the individual works in either period.

Formally, let the individual maximize $U(v_tW_t, h_tH_t, l_tL_t)$,[14] subject to $W_t + H_t + L_t = R$, where h_t and l_t are augmentation indexes for household production and leisure, with $h_0 = l_0 = 1$. The first-order conditions are $v_tU_1 = h_tU_2 = l_tU_3 = \lambda_t$.

If (W_0, H_0, L_0) is the maximizing decision at time zero and (W_t, H_t, L_t) at time t, what is the measure of the change in welfare? The change in utility can be linearly approximated as

$$U_1(v_tW_t - W_0) + U_2(h_tH_t - H_0) + U_3(l_tL_t - L_0)$$
$$= [U_1(W_t - W_0) + U_2(H_t - H_0) + U_3(L_t - L_0)]$$
$$+ [U_1(v_t - 1)W_t + U_2(h_t - 1)H_t + U_3(l_t - 1)L_t].$$

The first of the two terms is the substitution effect, which is approximately zero because with $v_0 = h_0 = l_0 = 1$, $U_1 = U_2 = U_3 = \lambda_0$ and $W_t + H_t + L_t = W_0 + H_0 + L_0 = R$. The second term is the income effect, the gain in utility we seek. Dividing by U_1, we convert the utility gain into its equivalent in market consumption:

$$(v_t - 1)W_t + (h_t - 1)H_t + (l_t - 1)L_t.$$

[14] We have assumed that work does not enter directly into the utility function. We do not consider complications that may arise if work is a direct source of satisfaction or pain, nor do we see any way to measure the marginal utility of work.

TABLE A.6
Rise in Three Price Indexes, 1929–65

	Ratio: 1965 to 1929	Average Annual Growth Rate
Consumption deflator	1.97	1.9%
Service deflator	2.06	2.0
Wage index	4.65	4.3

Source: NIP Table 8.1 (see note 6, above) and Table A.11 below.

Expressed as a ratio of base-period consumption R, this gives the results cited above: (A) if $h_t = l_t = 1$, (B) if $h_t = v_t$, $l_t = 1$, (C) if $h_t = l_t = v_t$.

Nonmarket activity. Housework is not directly productive of satisfaction, but rather yields a range of end products (meals, healthy children, gardens, etc.). Given the increase in household equipment and consumer durables, it would be surprising if nonmarket activities did not share in at least part of the advances in technologies that have raised productivity in the market economy.

The proper deflation of housework would be a base-weighted price of the bundle of home-produced services. In the absence of such an index, the closest measure is the deflator for the service component of consumption expenditures in the national accounts. This is compared with the total consumption deflator and the wage index in Table A.6.

It is clear that the price deflators for services and for consumption as a whole moved together over this period, while the wage index rose more than twice as fast. Table A.7 gives the growth of price indexes for important categories of consumption related to housework.

Leisure poses a deeper problem. To the extent that time itself is the final good — daydreaming, lounging, resting — then the conservative interpretation is indicated. But if leisure time is one among several inputs into a consumption process, then it may well have been augmented by technological progress embodied in the complementary inputs — television, boats, cars, sports equipment, etc.

A.3.2 Measurement. We are not aware of any reasonably comprehensive estimates of the use of time over the period 1929–65. Data on the average workweek are available and are used below. Ta-

TABLE A.7
Rise in Prices of Various Household Services, 1929–65

	Ratio: 1965 to 1929	Average Annual Growth Rate
Transportation	2.12	2.1%
Cleaning	2.06	2.0
Domestic service	3.39	3.4
Barbershops	3.03	3.1
Medical care	2.71	2.8
Purchased meals and beverages	2.35	2.4

Source: NIP Table 8.6 (see note 6, above). Note that the index of domestic service is an index of costs rather than a proper price index of output.

ble A.8 gives the results of a large sample survey conducted in 1954. We are doubtful about its reliability, but at present we have no choice but to base our estimates on this survey.

According to this survey leisure time of those surveyed amounted to about 47.6 hours per week for the men and 49.7 hours per week for the women. We will regard personal care and cost of work as instrumental maintenance items and exclude them from consumption. The

TABLE A.8
Use of Time, 1954
(average hours per day, between 6 A.M. to 11 P.M.)

	Men	Women
Gainful work	6.0	1.5
Cost of work	1.4	0.7
Personal care	0.6	0.9
Housework	2.2	6.7
Leisure	6.8	7.1

Note: Leisure includes time at restaurant, tavern; at friend's or relative's home; in games, sports, church; recreation at home; reading; and sleep during this seventeen-hour period.
Source: A Nationwide Study in Living Habits, cited in Sebastian de Grazia, *Of Time, Work, and Leisure,* New York, Twentieth Century Fund, 1962.

TABLE A.9

Principal Occupation of Population, 14 and Over,
Various Years, 1929–65

(*millions of persons*)

	Total Population	Em-ployed	Unem-ployed	Keeping House	School	Other
1929	88.0	47.9	1.5	28.1	6.0	4.5
1935	95.5	42.5	10.6	30.3	6.6	5.5
1945	106.7	64.3	1.0	27.8	4.8	8.8
1947	108.8	59.6	2.4	32.4	6.4	8.0
1954	117.7	64.3	3.6	33.9	6.3	9.6
1958	123.1	66.5	4.7	34.2	7.5	10.2
1965	137.6	74.6	3.5	35.6	11.1	12.8

Source: Economic Report of the President, 1967, Table B-20, for employed and unemployed. Other series from U.S. Department of Commerce, *Statistical Abstract of the United States,* various years; U.S. Department of Commerce, *Historical Statistics of the United States,* various editions. Since series are not always compatible, some adjustments have been made to link them. For 1929 and 1935, the last three columns are estimated from data on female population and employment, school enrollment, and population over 65 years, with the total constrained to equal total population.

important item other than leisure is housework, which takes 46.9 hours a week for women and 15.4 hours per week for men.

Table A.9 makes a breakdown of the population age 14 and over [15] by five time occupations for different years.

Table A.10 estimates the average hours of leisure and nonmarket activity for the five groups of the population described in Table A.9. Table A.11 shows the wage rates applicable to each group.

The general problem of valuation of housework and leisure time was discussed above. In addition, there are some special problems:

Unemployment: In general, time is to be valued at its opportunity cost, the wage rate. Should the unemployed be treated as having zero wage? Clearly this is not the proper treatment for the frictionally or voluntarily unemployed, whose opportunity cost should be close to the market wage rate. On the other hand, during the Great Depression, most unemployed persons could not have obtained work at anywhere near the prevailing wage. Our compromise is to treat unemployment

---

[15] Why do we exclude children under 14? Because the market value of their time is very low, not because we undervalue the joys of childhood.

TABLE A.10

Hours of Leisure and Nonmarket Work, Persons Over 14,
Various Years, 1929–65

(hours per week)

	Employed and Unemployed			Keeping House			School			Other		
	L	NM	Tot	L	NM	Tot	L	NM	Tot	L	NM	Tot
1929	39.4	15.4	54.8	49.7	46.9	96.6	50	13	63	50	10	60
1935	45.5	15.4	60.9	49.7	46.9	96.6	50	13	63	50	10	60
1945	43.1	15.4	58.5	49.7	46.9	96.6	50	13	63	50	10	60
1947	45.7	15.4	61.1	49.7	46.9	96.6	50	13	63	50	10	60
1954	47.6	15.4	63.0	49.7	46.9	96.6	50	13	63	50	10	60
1958	48.6	15.4	64.0	49.7	46.9	96.6	50	13	63	50	10	60
1965	48.1	15.4	63.5	49.7	46.9	96.6	50	13	63	50	10	60

L = leisure hours.
NM = nonmarket hours.
Tot = total hours.
Source: Hours of leisure are obtained by using the benchmark estimates for 1954 and then making estimates using data on average hours worked for other years. Thus the number of leisure hours for any year is obtained by subtracting from 47.6 (the number of hours of leisure for 1954) the difference in hours between the reference year and 1954. Hours data from John W. Kendrick, *Productivity Trends in the United States*, Princeton for NBER, 1961, Table A-X and A-VI. It is assumed that unemployed workers had the same number of hours of leisure and nonmarket work as employed workers. Further, it is assumed that nonmarket activity has stayed the same since 1929. Those keeping house were assumed to have no change from the total number of hours available in 1954 (96.6 per week). Arbitrary numbers were chosen for students and other persons.

as involuntary and thus assign a zero price to the normal working hours of the unemployed. On the other hand, we continue to value their leisure time at the going wage.[16]

Keeping house: The majority of those keeping house are women, and we thus choose the average hourly earnings for women as the proper valuation.

School: Since those in school are primarily under age 20, we use the wage for that age group as the proper valuation of school time.

[16] An alternate imputation is to value *all* time of unemployed workers at zero. For the depression year 1935, this lowers our final estimate of MEW (B variant) by 10 per cent. It makes very little difference for movements over the entire period.

TABLE A.11

Manufacturing Wage Rate and Wage Rate for Different Groups
in Population, Various Years, 1929–65

(*current dollars per hour*)

Year	Em-ployed	Unem-ployed	Females	Under 20 Years Old	Over 65 Years Old	Wage Index (1958 = 1.00)
1929	0.56	0.56	0.34	0.19	0.49	0.2654
1935	0.54	0.54	0.32	0.18	0.47	0.2559
1945	1.016	1.016	0.61	0.35	0.89	0.4815
1947	1.217	1.217	0.73	0.42	1.06	0.5768
1954	1.78	1.78	1.07	0.61	1.55	0.8436
1958	2.11	2.11	1.27	0.72	1.84	1.000
1965	2.61	2.61	1.57	0.89	2.28	1.237

Source: Basic wage data from *Economic Report of the President* and *Historical Statistics of the United States.* The basic figure is average hourly earnings in manufacturing, which is the only series available back to 1929. (This differs slightly but not appreciably from the ratio of total labor income to Kendrick's man-hour estimate.) Wage rates for females, and for those in the labor force who are under 20 or over 65 years old are calculated as a fraction of the manufacturing wage rate (these numbers being 0.58, 0.34, and 0.81). The data used to calculate the fractions are median incomes of persons who are year-round, full-time workers. Thus the ratio of median incomes of females to males is 4,560/7,814 = 0.58. (Data given in U.S. Department of Commerce, *Current Population Reports, Consumer Income,* Series P-60, No. 66, December 23, 1969, p. 90.)

The wage index is constructed from the data for employed workers with 1958 as the base.

"Other": The final category is "other persons," primarily retired. For this group, we choose the wage rate for persons over 65.

Finally in Table A.12 we calculate the total value of leisure, nonmarket activity, and the sum which we call the "time component" of MEW. Column 1 of Table A.12 gives the current dollar value of the three series. For the reasons given above, two alternative constant-dollar values are calculated for both leisure and nonmarket activity, one using the wage rate as deflator, the other using the consumption price index. Column 2 of Table A.12 shows the result if price deflation is used, while column 3 shows the result of using the wage deflator.

We feel that price deflation is probably superior for nonmarket activity, but that for leisure there is no general presumption. We have, therefore, proceeded with the three variants shown in Table A.12.

TABLE A.12
Value of Leisure and Nonmarket Activity, Various Years, 1929–65
(billions of dollars)

	Current Prices (1)	Deflated by Consumption Deflator (2)	Deflated by Wage Rates (3)
A. Leisure			
1929	90.1	162.9	339.5
1935	102.7	231.3	401.3
1945	217.0	331.8	450.7
1947	269.3	345.6	466.9
1954	441.4	477.2	523.2
1958	554.9	554.9	554.9
1965	775.5	712.8	626.9
B. Nonmarket Activity			
1929	47.4	85.7	178.6
1935	48.5	109.2	189.5
1945	99.7	152.4	207.1
1947	124.3	159.6	215.5
1954	195.6	211.5	231.9
1958	239.7	239.7	239.7
1965	321.4	295.4	259.8
C. Total, Time Component			
1929	137.5	248.6	518.1
1935	151.2	340.5	590.8
1945	316.7	484.2	657.8
1947	393.6	505.2	682.4
1954	637.0	688.7	755.1
1958	794.6	794.6	794.6
1965	1,096.9	1,008.2	886.7

Note: Column 1: For each group, total hours per week times total persons times hourly wage rate times 52, and sumed across all groups. Data are from Tables A.9, A.10, and A.11.

Column 2: Column 1 deflated by consumption deflator.

Column 3: Column 1 deflated by index of wage rate (last column of Table A.11).

TABLE

Preferred County Regression of the Logarithm

(figures in parentheses

Area	Con-stant (α_0)	Log of Popu-lation (α_1)	Log of Density (α_2)	Migra-tion Rate (α_3)	Log of % Urban Popu-lation (α_4)	Popu-lation Negro (α_5)
Mass., R.I.,	7.9 ‡	0.039 †	−0.020 *	0.00045	0.0595 *	−0.0089
Conn.	(17.1)	(1.89)	(0.92)	(0.24)	(0.93)	(−1.0)
New Mexico	2.85 †	0.093 *	−0.087 *	−0.00079	−0.073 †	−0.031 *
	(1.8)	(0.94)	(1.2)	(−0.58)	(1.5)	(1.0)
New York	7.7 ‡	0.010	0.035 ‡	0.0012 ‡	0.035 †	−0.011 ‡
	(15.3)	(0.65)	(2.98)	(0.25)	(1.3)	(2.9)
Wisconsin	7.74 ‡	−0.036 †	0.091 ‡	0.0029 ‡	0.035 ‡	−0.010
	(15.7)	(1.3)	(3.1)	(2.6)	(3.1)	(0.6)
Indiana	7.15 ‡	−0.0014	0.065 ‡	0.0017 ‡	0.0173 †	−0.0072 †
	(22.7)	(0.06)	(2.7)	(2.4)	(1.7)	(1.5)

NA = not available.
* Significant at 75 per cent confidence level.
† Significant at 90 per cent confidence level.
‡ Significant at 99 per cent confidence level.

Variant A: It is assumed that there has been no technological change in the time component, and deflation is therefore by wage rates.

Variant B: This is a hybrid, in which it is assumed that technological change has been occurring at the average rate for non-market activity, but that no technological change has taken place in leisure. For this variant, leisure is deflated by the wage index, while nonmarket activity is deflated by the consumption deflator.

Variant C: It is assumed that technological change has been occurring at the average rate for leisure and nonmarket activity, and both are therefore deflated by the consumption deflator.

For most of our discussion below and in the text, our preferred variant is B.

A.13
of Median Income on Selected Variables
are t ratios)

Population over 65 (α_6)	Log of Median Years of Schooling (α_7)	Log of Property Tax per Capita (α_8)	Log of Local Expenditures per Capita (α_9)	Observations	R^2	F Test	Mean of Dependent Variable	Standard Error of Estimate	Mean of Median Income per Household
−0.017	0.182 *	0.627 ‡	−0.603 ‡	25	.76	5.45	8.72	.061	$6,180
(0.021)	(0.73)	(4.13)	(3.09)						
−0.031 *	1.86 ‡	0.264 ‡	0.014	22	.91	14.4	8.38	.127	4,614
(0.93)	(4.21)	(1.70)	(0.035)						
−0.011 †	0.44 ‡	0.17 ‡	−0.22 ‡	62	.85	35.0	8.64	.540	5,761
(1.9)	(3.0)	(3.6)	(2.9)						
−0.020 ‡	0.383 ‡	−0.004	0.012	70	.88	49.4	8.46	.074	NA
(2.7)	(2.5)	(0.061)	(0.13)						
−0.020 ‡	0.413 ‡	0.114 ‡	−0.038	89	.87	60.6	8.52	.036	NA
(4.6)	(4.4)	(2.2)	(0.61)						

A.4 Disamenities and Externalities

In principle those social costs of economic activity that are not internalized as private costs should be subtracted in calculating our measures of economic welfare. The problems of measurement are formidable, and we have been able to do very little toward their solution.

One type of social cost not recorded in the national income accounts is the depletion of per capita stocks of environmental capital. Nonappropriated resources such as water and air are used and valued as if they were free, although reduction in the per capita stocks of these resources diminishes future sustainable consumption. If we had estimates of the value of environmental capital, we could add them to the national wealth estimates of Table A.3 and modify our calculations of MEW net investment accordingly. We have not been able to make this adjustment, but given the size of the other components of wealth, we do not believe it would be significant.

Some unrecorded social costs diminish economic welfare directly rather than through the depletion of environmental capital. The disamenities of urban life come to mind: pollution, litter, congestion, noise, insecurity, buildings and advertisements offensive to taste, etc. Failure to allow for these negative consumption items overstates not only the level but very possibly the growth of consumption. The fraction of the population exposed to these disamenities has increased, and the disamenities themselves may have become worse.

We have attempted to measure indirectly the costs of urbanization. Our measure relies on the assumption that people can still choose residential locations, urban or nonurban, high density or low density. Individuals and families on the margin of locational decisions will, we would expect, require higher incomes to live in densely populated cities than in small towns and rural areas. Urban areas do have higher wage rates and incomes. We interpret this differential as the "disamenity premium" compensating for living in less pleasant surroundings. From the estimated per capita income premium and the locational distribu-

TABLE A.14
Disamenity Estimates

Area	Total Population Effect $(\alpha_1 + \alpha_2)$	Urbanization Effect (α_4)
Massachusetts, Rhode Island, Connecticut	.019	.059
New Mexico	.006	−.073
New York	.045	.035
Wisconsin	.055	.035
Indiana	.064	.017
	Disamenity per Unit Change of Income, 1958 Prices	
	1.75 [a]	3.75 [b]

[a] The coefficient is $1.75 of average household income (1958 prices) per 1 million of population: 1.75 = 0.06 (5,421/180.7) (1.0/1.029), where 5,421 = median family income in the sample states, 180.7 is the population of the United States in millions, 1.0 and 1.029 are consumer deflators for 1958 and 1960, respectively, and 0.06 is the elasticity between income and population change.

[b] The coefficient for urbanization is $3.75 of average household income per percentage point rise in average urbanization: 3.75 = 0.04 (5,421/56.2) (1.0/1.029), where 56.2 is average urbanization, 0.04 is the elasticity between income and the urbanization effect, and all the other figures are as described in note a, above.

TABLE A.15
Corrections for Disamenities of Population and Urbanization, Various Years, 1929–65

	1929	1935	1945	1947	1954	1958	1965
1. Households (no. of mill.)	29.5	32.5	38.9	40.3	46.9	51.0	59.0
2. Disposable personal income per household (1958 prices)	5,105	4,055	5,904	5,409	5,934	6,251	7,389
3. Per cent urbanization	56.2	56.3	58.0	58.6	61.4	62.2	65.1
4. Total population (no. of mill.)	121.8	127.3	140.0	144.1	163.0	174.9	194.6
5. Population density (persons per square mile)	40.3	42.1	46.5	47.9	53.9	57.8	64.4
6. Total correction per household (1958 prices)	425.1	435.1	464.7	474.4	517.2	541.1	586.6
7. Total correction (billions of dollars, 1958 prices)	12.5	14.1	18.1	19.1	24.3	27.6	34.6

Source (for NIP, see note 6, above):

Line

1   *Historical Statistics* and *Statistical Abstract,* various years. Linear interpolation is used to estimate households in noncensus years.

2   Personal disposable income in 1958 prices (NIP Table 2.1) divided by line 1.

3   Same as line 1.

4   *Economic Report of the President, 1968,* Table B-21.

5   Line 4 divided by 3,022,387 square miles.

6   Equals $1.75 times line 4 plus $3.75 times line 3.

7   Equals line 6 times line 1.

tion of the population we can compute an aggregate correction and observe its changes over time.

Urban income differentials also reflect, of course, technological productivity advantages. The uncorrected national accounts claim all the gains in productivity associated with urbanization; our correction removes some of them on the ground that they merely offset disamenities. We would not be justified in cancelling out income differentials which are still inducing migration. We have therefore allowed for observed migration and estimated an equilibrium zero-migration differential. We have also attempted to standardize for other factors affecting locational decision besides density and for other sources of income differences.

Our estimates are based on a single cross section, the 1960 census. Consequently we do not know whether the disamenity premium has

TABLE A.16

Measures of Economic Welfare, Actual and
Sustainable, Various Years, 1929–65

(*billions of dollars, 1958 prices, except lines 14–19, as noted*)

	1929	1935	1945	1947	1954	1958	1965
1 Personal consumption, national income and product accounts	139.6	125.5	183.0	206.3	255.7	290.1	397.7
2 Private instrumental expenditures	−10.3	−9.2	−9.2	−10.9	−16.4	−19.9	−30.9
3 Durable goods purchases	−16.7	−11.5	−12.3	−26.2	−35.5	−37.9	−60.9
4 Other household investment	−6.5	−6.3	−9.1	−10.4	−15.3	−19.6	−30.1
5 Services of consumer capital imputation	24.9	17.8	22.1	26.7	37.2	40.8	62.3
6 Imputation for leisure							
B	339.5	401.3	450.7	466.9	523.2	554.9	626.9
A	339.5	401.3	450.7	466.9	523.2	554.9	626.9
C	162.9	231.3	331.8	345.6	477.2	554.9	712.8
7 Imputation for nonmarket activities							
B	85.7	109.2	152.4	159.6	211.5	239.7	295.4
A	178.6	189.5	207.1	215.5	231.9	239.7	259.8
C	85.7	109.2	152.4	159.6	211.5	239.7	295.4
8 Disamenity correction	−12.5	−14.1	−18.1	−19.1	−24.3	−27.6	−34.6
9 Government consumption	0.3	0.3	0.4	0.5	0.5	0.8	1.2
10 Services of government capital imputation	4.8	6.4	8.9	10.0	11.7	14.0	16.6
11 Total consumption = actual MEW							
B	548.8	619.4	768.8	803.4	948.3	1,035.3	1,243.6
A	641.7	699.7	823.5	859.3	968.7	1,035.3	1,208.0
C	372.2	449.4	649.9	682.1	902.3	1,035.3	1,329.5
12 MEW net investment	−5.3	−46.0	−52.5	55.3	13.0	12.5	−2.5
13 Sustainable MEW							
B	543.5	573.4	716.3	858.7	961.3	1,047.8	1,241.1
A	636.4	653.7	771.0	914.6	981.7	1,047.8	1,205.5
C	366.9	403.4	597.4	737.4	915.3	1,047.8	1,327.0
14 Population (no. of mill.)	121.8	127.3	140.5	144.7	163.0	174.9	194.6

(*continued*)

Table A.16 (concluded)

	1929	1935	1945	1947	1954	1958	1965
Actual MEW per capita							
15 Dollars							
B	4,506	4,866	5,472	5,552	5,818	5,919	6,391
A	5,268	5,496	5,861	5,938	5,943	5,919	6,208
C	3,056	3,530	4,626	4,714	5,536	5,919	6,832
16 Index (1929 = 100)							
B	100.0	108.0	121.4	123.2	129.1	131.4	141.8
A	100.0	104.3	111.3	112.7	112.8	112.4	117.8
C	100.0	115.5	151.4	154.3	181.2	193.7	223.6
Sustainable MEW per capita							
17 Dollars							
B	4,462	4,504	5,098	5,934	5,898	5,991	6,378
A	5,225	5,135	5,488	6,321	6,023	5,991	6,195
C	3,012	3,169	4,252	5,096	5,615	5,991	6,819
18 Index (1929 = 100)							
B	100.0	100.9	114.3	133.0	132.2	134.3	142.9
A	100.0	98.3	105.0	121.0	115.3	114.7	118.6
C	100.0	105.2	141.2	169.2	186.4	198.9	226.4
19 Per capita NNP							
Dollars	1,945	1,205	2,401	2,038	2,305	2,335	2,897
1929 = 100	100.0	78.0	155.4	131.9	149.2	151.1	187.5

Source (for NIP, see note 6, above):

Line
1   NIP Table 1.2, line 2.
2   NIP Table 2.5, line 52 (personal business), plus one-fifth of line 60 (transportation), deflated by consumption deflator, NIP Table 8.1, line 2.
3   NIP Table 1.1, line 3, deflated by consumption deflator, NIP Table 8.1, line 2.
4   NIP Table 2.5, lines 42 plus 93 less 44, all deflated by consumption deflator, NIP Table 8.1, line 2.
5   Table A.4.
6   Table A.12, part A. Variants B and C from column 3; C, from column 2.
7   Table A.12, part B. Variants B and C from column 2; A, from column 2.
8   Table A.15.
9   Table A.1, line 1.
10 Table A.4.
11 Sum of lines 1–10.
12 Table A.5, line 11.
13 Line 10 plus line 11.
14 *Economic Report of the President, 1971,* Table C-21, p. 221.
15 Line 11 divided by line 14.
17 Line 13 divided by line 14.
19 NNP (NIP Table 1.9) divided by GNP deflator (NIP Table 8.1) times population (Table A.15, line 4).

increased over time. We have simply applied the 1960 premium to population distributions 1929–65.

The unit of observation is the county. It was desired to include sparsely populated areas, and this would not be possible with cities or standard metropolitan statistical areas. The basic data are from the U.S. Department of Commerce *City and County Data Book,* 1960. Regressions were run separately across the counties in each of four states, and in three New England states as a unit. This procedure was followed because we thought that pooling across states and regions would introduce additional sources of variation in locational decision and income choice and obscure the density effects we were seeking to estimate.

The regressions are reported in Table A.13. The dependent variable is the log of median family income for the county. The relevant coefficients are α_1, α_2, and α_4, referring to county population, density, and per cent of county population in urban areas. The other regression variables are included to allow for other sources of income differences. Table A.14 summarizes the regression results for the population variables and shows the values used in the MEW calculations carried out in Table A.15.

The disamenity adjustment is not insubstantial: In 1965 it was about 8 per cent of average family disposable income. If the population were completely urbanized, the adjustment would be about one-third of income. But the correction as a fraction of income has not risen since 1929. Although the population has become more urban and more dense, incomes have grown relative to the disamenity differential.

A.5   Estimates of MEW

We now assemble the components of MEW in Table A.16, which is the same as text Table 1. We also show, in Table A.17, a reconciliation of MEW and GNP. In Table A.18, we show growth rates of NNP and of the three variants of MEW-S. These four series are plotted in Figure A.3.

MEW looks quite different from NNP. It is roughly twice as large. Our preferred variant of MEW-S — variant B, which deflates nonmarket activity by the consumption price index and leisure by the wage rate — has grown somewhat more slowly than NNP: 2.3 per cent per annum compared with 3.0 per cent. The more optimistic variant C has risen faster than NNP. Even the most conservative estimate of MEW-S,

TABLE A.17
Gross National Product and MEW, Various Years, 1929–65
(billions of dollars, 1958 prices)

	1929	1935	1945	1947	1954	1958	1965
1. Gross national product	203.6	169.5	355.2	309.9	407.0	447.3	617.8
2. Capital consumption, NIPA	−20.0	−20.0	−21.9	−18.3	−32.5	−38.9	−54.7
3. Net national product, NIPA	183.6	149.5	333.3	291.6	374.5	408.4	563.1
4. NIPA final output reclassified as regrettables and intermediates							
a. Government	−6.7	−7.4	−146.3	−20.8	−57.8	−56.4	−63.2
b. Private	−10.3	−9.2	−9.2	−10.9	−16.4	−19.9	−30.9
5. Imputations for items not included in NIPA							
a. Leisure	339.5	401.3	450.7	466.9	523.2	554.9	626.9
b. Nonmarket activity	85.7	109.2	152.4	159.6	211.5	239.7	295.4
c. Disamenities	−12.5	−14.1	−18.1	−19.1	−24.3	−27.6	−34.6
d. Services of public and private capital	29.7	24.2	31.0	36.7	48.9	54.8	78.9
6. Additional capital consumption	−19.3	−33.4	−11.7	−50.8	−35.2	−27.3	−92.7
7. Growth requirement	−46.1	−46.7	−65.8	+5.4	−63.1	−78.9	−101.8
8. Sustainable MEW	543.6	573.4	716.3	858.6	961.3	1,047.7	1,241.1

Source (for NIP, see note 6, above):

Line
1 NIP Table 1.2, line 1.
2 Table A.5, line 6.
3 Line 1 minus line 2.
4a Table A.1, line 3 plus line 4.
4b Table A.16, line 2.
5a Table A.16, line 6.
5b Table A.16, line 7.
5c Table A.16, line 8.
5d Table A.4.
6 Table A.5, line 9 minus line 6.
7 Table A.5, line 10.
8 Sum of lines 3–7; equals Table A.16, line 13.

TABLE A.18

Rates of Growth of NNP and of Sustainable MEW,
Various Periods, 1929–65

(*average compound growth rate, per cent per year*)

	1929–47	1947–65	1929–65
Total			
NNP	2.6	3.6	3.1
MEW variant			
A	2.1	1.5	1.8
B	2.6	2.0	2.3
C	4.0	3.3	3.6
Per capita			
NNP	1.4	2.0	1.7
MEW variant			
A	1.1	−0.1	0.5
B	1.6	0.4	1.0
C	2.3	1.6	2.3
Population	0.96	1.65	1.3

Source: Tables A.16 and A.17.

variant A, shows progress, though only at a rate of 0.5 per cent per year.

The modifications of the national accounts which make the most difference are the omissions of regrettables and the imputations for leisure and nonmarket work.

The net MEW investment rate was negative before the Second World War and mainly positive since. Since 1945 sustainable MEW has, in the main, exceeded actual MEW (Figure A.4). We have been investing enough to move the economy to a higher consumption path.

A.6 Reliability of the Estimates

In national accounting, reliability cannot be calculated like statistical sampling error but only judged, for the most part subjectively, by those familiar with the data and the adjustments made in them. We have attempted to estimate very roughly the reliability of our measure of MEW and of its components. These judgments are presented in Table A.19.

FIGURE A.3
Per Capita Net National Product (NNP) and Per Capita Sustainable
MEW, 1929–65
(*1958 prices*)

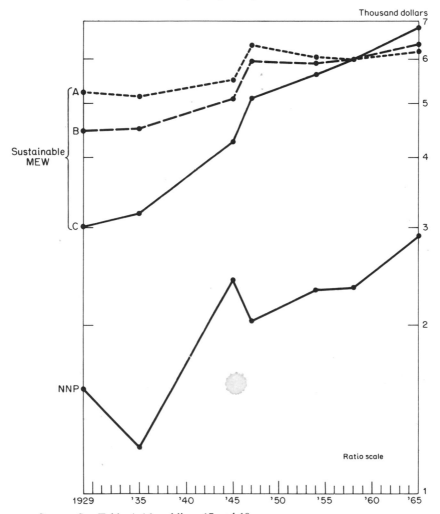

Source: See Table A.16 and lines 17 and 19.

FIGURE A.4
Per Capita Net National Product (NNP) and Per Capita Actual MEW,
1929–65
(*1958 prices*)

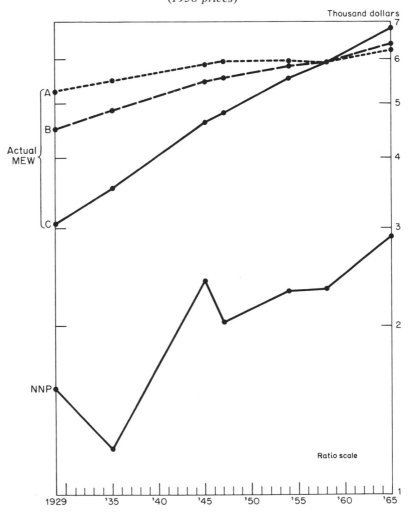

Source: See Table A.16, lines 15 and 19.

TABLE A.19
Reliability of the Estimates of MEW

Item	Reliability
Consumption expenditures in national accounts	low error
Corrections for	
Instrumental expenditures	medium error
Capital consumption	high error
Growth requirement	high error
MEW net investment	very high error
Imputations for	
Capital services	high error
Leisure	very high error
Nonmarket activity	very high error
Disamenity	very high error
Totals	
GNP	low error
MEW	
Excluding time component	medium error
With time component	high error

Source: Authors' judgment.

We have used as a benchmark the reliability of the gross national product estimates, which we call (for reference) "low error."[17] An item with "medium error" is one with a percentage error we feel to be about twice the percentage error of the GNP. "High error" is about five times the percentage error of GNP. "Very high error" is about ten times the percentage error of GNP.

The sources of unreliability lie both in the data (especially in the case of the time components of MEW) and in the concepts used (such as the proper deflator for leisure or the proper regression for calculating the disamenity premium). There are no independent estimates of comparable totals, as is sometimes the case in the income and product accounts. Totals therefore have all the unreliabilities that their components in combination contribute.

[17] Although no official estimate of the unreliability of GNP exists in the United States, the official estimate in the United Kingdom is that three percentage points either way includes a 90 per cent confidence interval. (See Rita Maurice, ed., *National Accounts Statistics, Sources and Methods,* London, Central Statistical Office, 1969, pp. 42 and 52.)

We must in all candor recognize that in moving away from the conventional accounting framework, we must accept sizable losses in the precision of the estimates.

APPENDIX B: NATURAL RESOURCES

B.1   The Role of Natural Resources in Economic Growth

In this appendix we consider the importance of natural resources in measured economic growth. In comparison with the usual neoclassical growth model, the laws of production are more complex. There are not simply constant returns to scale in capital and labor. The easiest way to view the problem is to assume a constant-returns-to-scale aggregate production function of the form

$$Y = F(A_K K, A_L L, A_R R) \qquad (B.1)$$

where Y is output, and K, L, and R are the services from capital, labor, and natural resources, respectively. All technological change is assumed to be factor-augmenting, and A_i is the augmentation level of factor i.

In general, resources might be renewable and augmentable, like capital, or exhaustible, like stocks of minerals. But we shall confine ourselves to the case typified by "land," where the stock is constant — neither augmentable nor destructible — and the services are proportional to the stock.

We can take the logarithmic derivative of (B.1) to obtain:

$$\hat{Y} = \xi_K(\hat{A}_K + \hat{K}) + \xi_L(\hat{A}_L + \hat{L}) + \xi_R(\hat{A}_R + \hat{R}) \qquad (B.2)$$

where hats over variables represent proportional rates of growth, and ξ_i is the elasticity of output with respect to factor i.

Since our main interest is the movement of per capita quantities, we define y as per capita income Y/L, k as capital per head K/L, and r as land per head R/L. From (B.2) we derive

$$\hat{y} = \hat{Y} - \hat{L} = \hat{A} + \xi_K(\hat{K} - \hat{L}) + \xi_R(\hat{R} - \hat{L}) + (\xi_K + \xi_R + \xi_L - 1)\hat{L}$$

where $\hat{A} = \hat{A}_K \xi_K + \hat{A}_L \xi_L + \hat{A}_R \xi_R$.

On the assumption of constant returns to scale, the sum of the elasticities of the three factors is unity. If $\hat{L}$ is the constant n, then $\hat{r} = \hat{R} - \hat{L} = -n$, and we have

$$\hat{y} = \hat{A} + \xi_K \hat{k} - \xi_R n, \qquad (B.3)$$

and

$$\hat{k} = (sy/k) - n. \tag{B.4}$$

The production function (B.1) can be converted to the intensive form

$$y = A_L f(a_k k, a_r r) = A_L F(A_K K / A_L L, 1, A_R R / A_L L).$$

Balanced growth could occur with constant elasticities ξ_i, constant rates of technical progress, and a constant capital-output ratio k/y. The balanced growth rate is obtained by letting $\hat{k} = \hat{y}$ in (B.3). It is $(\hat{A} - \xi_R n)/(1 - \xi_K)$. The drag due to resource limitation is indicated by the second term in the numerator, as well as by the possibility that ξ_K is smaller than it would be in a two-factor economy.

The share of natural resource owners in national income appears to have fallen over time. This trend is not compatible with balanced growth, and there are several possible interpretations of it. One is the following combination of circumstances: The elasticity of substitution resources for the other two factors taken jointly is greater than 1, and the *effective* quantity of resources per effective worker, $a_r r$, is declining. This implies that the elasticity of output with respect to resources, ξ_R, is falling, and therefore that the drag on growth is progressively diminishing.

A second interpretation is quite the opposite: The elasticity of substitution is less than 1, but effective resources per effective worker are growing, thanks to the speed of resource-augmenting progress.

A third possible mechanism is a shift in demand away from resource-intensive goods, as a result either of income or of price effects. This mechanism cannot be easily described in a one-sector aggregative model. But price-induced shifts of demand are similar in effect to price-induced shifts of factor proportions. A high elasticity of substitution will lower the income shares of resource owners. Inelasticity of demand for resource-intensive products with respect to income growth has the same qualitative effects as rapid land-augmenting progress.

To the central question — How important are natural resources in measured growth? — we seem to get an unambiguous answer: less important than they were. Table B.1, from Denison, indicates that the share of land declined from about 9 per cent to 3 per cent from 1900 to 1950.[18] Denison concludes that while land slowed down the growth rate 0.11 per cent per annum for the period 1909–29, this drag was only

---

[18] *Sources*, p. 30.

TABLE B.1

Shares of Factors in National Income, Various Periods, 1909–58

Period	National Income	Labor	Land	Total	Reproducible Capital Goods				
					Nonfarm Residential Structures	Other Structures and Equipment	Inventories	U.S. Holdings of Private Assets Abroad	Less: Foreign Holdings of U.S. Private Assets
1909–13	100.0	69.5	8.9	21.6	3.3	13.9	4.6	0.4	.6
1914–18	100.0	67.0	8.8	24.2	3.5	15.3	5.3	0.4	.3
1919–23	100.0	69.5	7.0	23.5	3.4	14.8	4.7	0.8	.2
1924–28	100.0	69.7	6.4	23.9	4.3	14.6	4.3	0.9	.2
1929–33 [a]	100.0	69.2	6.2	24.6	4.5	15.3	4.2	1.0	.4
1934–38 [a]	100.0	70.4	5.6	24.0	3.6	15.6	4.3	0.8	.3
1939–43 [a]	100.0	72.1	4.9	23.0	2.8	15.5	4.3	0.6	.2
1944–48 [a]	100.0	74.9	4.0	21.1	2.2	14.6	3.9	0.5	.1
1949–53	100.0	74.5	3.4	22.1	2.5	15.4	3.8	0.5	.1
1954–58	100.0	77.3	3.0	19.7	3.0	13.1	3.0	0.7	.1
1909–58 [a]	100.0	71.4	5.8	22.8	3.3	14.9	4.2	0.6	.2
1909–29	100.0	68.9	7.7	23.4	3.7	14.6	4.8	0.6	.3
1929–58 [a]	100.0	73.0	4.5	22.5	3.1	15.0	3.9	0.7	.2

Source: Reproduced from Denison, *Sources,* p. 30.

[a] For 1930 through 1940 and 1942 through 1946 these represent interpolated distributions, not the actual distribution for those dates. See text.

0.05 per cent for 1929–57 and would fall slightly more for the next twenty years.[19] In subsequent work, Denison has also examined the extent to which differences in supplies of land and natural resources can account for differences in productivity and growth between the United States and Western European countries. He finds the differences negligible.[20]

A closer look at specific products which are resource-intensive confirms the general suspicion that resources have not been a drag. In a careful study of the relative costs and prices of major categories of

[19] *Ibid.,* p. 270.

[20] See Edward F. Denison, *Why Growth Rates Differ,* Washington, D.C., Brookings, 1967, Chap. 14. The difference ranges between 0.5 and 0.6 per cent of per capita national income.

resource-intensive goods, Barnett and Morse conclude that, with the exception of forestry products, none appears to have become relatively more scarce than goods in general.[21] They examine reasons for this paradox and show that the most important reason is pervasive technological change. Moreover, in those resource-using industries where technology has not come to the rescue of scarcity, substitution of other goods has been significant (substitution away from lead and zinc, from forestry products, from animal power in agriculture).[22]

B.2   Simulations of Three-Factor Production Functions

Our brief review of historical tendencies in resource industries has led us to conclude tentatively that natural resources have not become an increasing drag on economic growth. One possible explanation for this result is that technology allows ample means for substituting away from increasingly scarce natural resources.

In an attempt to make this speculation more concrete, we have studied several three-factor aggregate production functions. Although two-factor (labor-capital) production functions have been widely studied, there does not appear to be comparable work on three-factor (labor-capital-land) functions. Moreover, the only analytical results available are for production functions with constant partial elasticities of substitution between different factors. Consequently, our first step was to examine different functional forms and parameter combinations to see which seemed to exhibit plausible behavior. The final choice between the simulations was on the basis of a comparison of the simulated results with the "revised stylized facts" of growth reviewed above.

B.2.1   Parameters.   Four functional forms were tested:

$$Y = [\alpha_1 (A_K K)^{-\rho} + \alpha_2 (A_L L)^{-\rho} + \alpha_3 (A_R R)^{-\rho}]^{-1/\rho} \qquad \text{(PF1)}$$

$$Y = \{\alpha_1 [(A_K K)^{1/4} (A_L L)^{3/4}]^{-\rho} + \alpha_2 (A_R R)^{-\rho}\}^{-1/\rho} \qquad \text{(PF2)}$$

$$Y = (\alpha_1 \{[\beta_1 (A_K K)^{1/2} + \beta_2 (A_L L)^{1/2}]^{1/2}\}^{-\rho} + \alpha_2 (A_R R)^{-\rho})^{-1/\rho} \quad \text{(PF3)}$$

$$Y = (\alpha_1 \{[\beta_1 (A_K K)^{-1} + \beta_2 (A_L L)^{-1}]^{-1}\}^{-\rho} + \alpha_2 (A_R R)^{-\rho})^{-1/\rho} \quad \text{(PF4)}$$

---

[21] See Harold J. Barnett and Chandler Morse, *Scarcity and Growth*, Baltimore, Johns Hopkins University Press, 1963, Part III. The other broad sectors were agriculture, extractive industries, and minerals.

[22] "A rough calculation based on Btu's of mineral fuel indicates that if the United States today has to rely upon work animals for its 'horsepower,' the feed would require 15 to 30 times as many acres of cropland as are in use in the country" (*ibid.*, p. 185).

The first one is a general three-factor production function with constant elasticity of substitution (CES). The others are two-stage CES functions, in which production depends on two factors, resources and a capital-labor composite. In PF2 the capital-labor composite is a Cobb-Douglas function of capital and labor, with assumed elasticities of $1/4$ for labor and $3/4$ for capital. In PF3 and PF4 the composite is itself a CES function of the two "neoclassical" factors, with different elasticities of substitution between them. Unlike PF1, the two-stage functions imply a different partial elasticity of substitution between capital and labor from that between resources and the other two inputs.

In summary, the assumed elasticity between (K, L) and R is the same for all four production functions, namely, $1/(1 + \rho)$. The assumed elasticity between K and L is as follows:

| PF1 | $1/(1 + \rho)$ | PF3 | 2 |
| PF2 | 1 | PF4 | 1/2 |

The parameter values tested in simulations were as follows: For ρ, $-9/10$, $-1/2$, $-1/3$, 1. For the rate of labor-augmenting progress, $(g_A)_L$; the rate of capital-augmenting progress, $(g_A)_K$; and the rate of resource-augmenting progress, $(g_A)_R$, the values are 0.0, 0.015, and 0.03.

The numerical specifications were completed with the following parameters: $\alpha_1 = 0.9$; $\alpha_2 = 0.1$; $\beta_1 = 0.25$; $\beta_2 = 0.75$; $s =$ net savings rate $(\Delta K/Y) = 0.1$; $g_L =$ natural growth rate of labor $= 0.01$; $g_R =$ growth rate of resource input $= 0.0$. All values were indexed at 100 at time $t = 0$.

Altogether there were 405 specifications, differing in the form of the function (PF1–PF4) and in the numerical values of their parameters. Each case was simulated for 300 "years." The results were compared with the following stylized facts:

Factor shares are labor 0.73; capital, 0.22; resources, 0.05 (Denison, *Sources*).
Capital growth exceeds output growth by 1 per cent per year.
Output growth is 3.5 per cent per year.
The marginal product of capital (MPK) is constant at 0.15.

Simulations were scored by their conformity to these "facts." Two scoring procedures were used.

The first was based on an arbitrarily weighted sum of squared deviations of simulated results from the facts:

$(L$ share $- 0.73)^2 + (K$ share $- 0.22)^2$

$$+ 2(R \text{ share} - 0.05)^2 + 3[(g_K - g_Y) - (-0.01)]^2$$

$$+ 10(g_Y - 0.035)^2 + 0.2(MPK - 0.15)^2. \quad \text{(B.5)}$$

For each simulation, this sum was computed for each period, and its minimum value found. The minimum value was Score I for the simulation. The lower the score, the more acceptable the simulation.

Score II was simply the number of individual criteria met in the year 100 of the simulation, to a maximum of 10 criteria. The criteria were:

$$
\begin{array}{rll}
\text{(i)} & (g_K - g_Y) \text{ in } [-0.02, 0.005] & \text{(B.6)} \\
\text{(ii)} & (g_{MPL} - g_Y) \text{ in } [-0.01, 0.01] & \\
\text{(iii)} & g_{MPK} \text{ in } [0.02, 0.02] & \\
\text{(iv)} & g \text{ (share of labor)} \geqq 0 & \\
\text{(v)} & \text{share of labor in } [0.6, 0.8] & \\
\text{(vi)} & g \text{ (share of } K) \text{ in } [-0.005, 0.005] & \\
\text{(vii)} & \text{share of } K \text{ in } [0.15, 0.30] & \\
\text{(viii)} & \text{(share of } R) \leqq 0 & \\
\text{(ix)} & \text{share of } R \text{ in } [0.02, 0.10] & \\
\text{(x)} & g_Y \text{ in } [0.03, 0.04] &
\end{array}
$$

Conditions (v), (vii), (ix), (i), and (x) in (B.6) are analogous to the first five terms in (B.5) in that order.

B.2.2   Results.   The two scoring functions are quite consistent. Score I ranged from 0.001183 to more than 3.0. The 51 lowest scores, ranging from 0.001183 to 0.003998, are analyzed below. None of the 405 cases scored 10 on the second test; ten scored 9. All ten of these cases are among the 51 cited above and listed in Table B.2, below. Other summary compilations appear in Table B.3, below.

Two fairly definite conclusions emerge from these simulations. The elasticity of substitution between resources and the capital-labor composite is greater than 1 in all 51 cases. Secondly, the partial elasticity of substitution between K and L is greater than 1 in the top seven cases, and equal to 1 (Cobb-Douglas) in 35 of the next following cases. Only one out of the 102 substitution elasticities in these 51 cases is less than unity.

The findings relating to the rates of labor- and capital-augmenting technical change are somewhat clouded since in the Cobb-Douglas case factor-augmenting change is indistinguishable from Hicks-neutral

TABLE B.2
Fifty-One Best-scoring Simulations

PF	$\sigma_{(K,L),R}$ $=\dfrac{1}{1+\rho}$	$\sigma_{K,L}$	$(g_A)_R$	$(g_A)_K$	$(g_A)_L$	Score I
1	1.5	1.5	0	0	.03	.001183
(1,3)	2	2	0	0	.03	.001250
1	1.5	1.5	.03	0	.03	.001283
3	1.5	2	0	0	.03	.001303
(1,3)	2	2	.015	0	.03	.001325
3	10	2	.015	0	.03	.001344
(1,3)	2	2	.03	0	.03	.001456
2	2	1	.03	0	.03	.001516
1	10	10	0	0	.03	.001531
3	10	2	0	0	.03	.001535
2	1.5	1	.03	0	.03	.001559
2	2	1	0	0	.03	.001634
2	10	1	.03	.03	.015	.001642
2	1.5	1	.015	.03	.015	.001646
2	10	1	.015	.03	.015	.001688
2	10	1	.015	0	.03	.001704
2	1.5	1	0	0	.03	.001719
2	2	1	.015	.03	.015	.001723
2	2	1	.03	.03	.015	.001732
1	10	10	.015	0	.03	.001753
2	2	1	0	.03	.015	.001799
3	1.5	2	.03	0	.03	.001828
2	2	1	.015	0	.03	.001872
2	10	1	0	.03	.015	.001887
2	1.5	1	.03	.015	.03	.001975
2	10	1	0	0	.03	.001994
3	10	2	.03	0	.03	.002125
3	1.5	2	.015	0	.03	.002147
2	10	1	.03	0	.03	.002171
1	1.5	1.5	.015	0	.03	.002208
2	2	1	.03	.015	.03	.002272
2	1.5	1	.015	0	.03	.002285
2	1.5	1	0	.015	.03	.002302
2	1.5	1	0	.03	.015	.002346
2	1.5	1	.015	.015	.015	.002382
1	10	10	.03	0	.03	.002407
2	2	1	.015	.015	.03	.002441
2	1.5	1	.03	.03	.015	.002480

(continued)

Table B.2 (concluded)

PF	$\sigma_{(K,L),R}$ $= \dfrac{1}{1 + \rho}$	$\sigma_{K,L}$	$(g_A)_R$	$(g_A)_K$	$(g_A)_L$	Score I
2	2	1	.015	.015	.015	.002759
2	2	1	0	.015	.03	.002779
2	10	1	.03	.015	.03	.002795
2	1.5	1	.015	.015	.03	.003123
2	1.5	1	.03	.03	.03	.003155
2	10	1	.015	.015	.03	.003288
2	10	1	.015	.015	.015	.003360
2	1.5	1	0	.015	.015	.003462
2	2	1	0	.015	.015	.003588
4	1.5	0.5	.015	0	.015	.003630
2	1.5	1	.015	0	.015	.003634
2	10	1	0	.015	.015	.003883
2	1.5	1	0	.03	.03	.003907

(separable) technical change. There is, however, some reason to favor an estimate of $(g_A)_L$ of 0.03 and of $(g_A)_K$ of 0.0. Of the sixteen cases in Table B.1 which are not Cobb-Douglas, fifteen have $[(g_A)_K, (g_A)_L] = (0, 0.03)$. In 26 of the 35 Cobb-Douglas cases, $(1/4)(g_A)_K + (3/4)(g_A)_L$ was in the range $[2 - (1/8), 2 - (5/8)]$.

No conclusions are possible regarding the growth rate of resource-augmenting change. In all cases effective resources grow less rapidly than effective capital plus effective labor; therefore, with $\sigma_{(K,L),N}$ greater than unity the share of resources declines. If higher rates of g_R had been chosen, this conclusion might have been reversed.

One final note of interest is that the simulations *did* produce a declining capital-output ratio. Since the "apparent" decline of the capital-output ratio has been a puzzle to analysts, it is of some interest to see how this arises in the present model. As is well known, the capital-output ratio in balanced growth is the ratio of the saving rate to the rate of growth of the exogenous factor (usually labor). In a three-factor model, the composite exogenous factor is the combination of labor and resources, weighted by their relative shares. But inputs of resources are growing more slowly than labor inputs, and the share of resources is declining relative to labor's. Therefore, the growth rate of the composite exogenous factor is speeding up over time and the equilibrium capital-output ratio is falling.

B.2.3 The Next Fifty Years? Under the assumption that the models which best correspond to the stylized facts will apply to the future, we can draw inferences about the next few decades. All of the best simulations indicate the same trends; the exact numbers given below are from the best Cobb-Douglas case (PF2), which had $\sigma_{(K,L),R} = 2$, and $[(g_A)_R, (g_A)_K, (g_A)_L] = [0.03, 0, 0.03]$, beginning at year 150.

Briefly, very little changes. The K/Y ratio declines slightly (2.53 to 2.52), while shares of capital and labor increase slightly at the expense of resources (0.237 to 0.240, 0.711 to 0.719, 0.052 to 0.041, respectively). The marginal product of capital rises (0.0936 to 0.0952). The growth rate of output rises slightly (0.0397 to 0.0398), while the rate of change of wages (marginal product per natural worker) approaches 0.03 (up from 0.0296 to 0.0297).

B.3 Production Models Including Natural Resources: Econometric Estimates

The simulations described in the last section are quite optimistic about the effects of natural resources on future growth. They imply that growth will accelerate rather than slow down even as natural resources become more scarce in the future. Since the models used there are only suggestive, it is perhaps useful to check the results with a more formal approach.

One of the best simulations was of the following form, PF2: [23]

$$Y = \{\alpha_1[(A_K K)^\epsilon(A_L L)^{1-\epsilon}]^{-\rho} + \alpha_2(A_R R)^{-\rho}\}^{-1/\rho} \qquad (B.7)$$

where ϵ was assumed to be $1/4$. In this specification, capital and labor are combined with an elasticity of substitution of 1, while the composite capital-labor factor and natural resources are combined with an elasticity of substitution of $1/(1 + \rho)$. Let us designate the composite factor as:

$$N = K^\epsilon L^{1-\epsilon} e^{ht} \qquad (B.8)$$

where $h = (g_A)_K \epsilon + (g_A)_L(1 - \epsilon)$.

One way to calculate ρ is as follows. The ratio between the shares of the composite factor and natural resources is:

$$z = \frac{\text{share of } N}{\text{share of } R} = \frac{\alpha_1}{\alpha_2}\left(\frac{R}{N}\right)^\rho e^{\lambda \rho t} \qquad (B.9)$$

where $\lambda = (g_A)_R - h$.

[23] This form won 15 of the top 24 places on Score I.

TABLE B.3
Distribution of Fifty-one Lowest Scores

By Elasticity of Substitution Between Capital and Labor		By Rates of Factor-Augmenting Technical Change			
$\sigma_{(K,L),R}$	No.	Rate	$(g_A)_R$	$(g_A)_K$	$(g_A)_L$
0.5	0	0	17	26	0
1.5	21	.015	19	14	17
2.0	14	.03	15	11	34
10.0	17				

By Production Function			By Combinations of Rates of Technical Change	
Function	$\sigma_{K,L}$	No.	$(g_A)_R, (g_A)_K, (g_A)_L$	No.
PF1	a	9 b	(0, 0, .03)	8
PF2	1.0	35	(.015, 0, .03)	8
PF3	2.0	9 b	(.03, 0, .03)	8
PF4	0.5	1	All others c	27
				51

a Same as $\sigma_{(K,L),R}$.
b In three cases, PF1 and PF3 are identical.
c Fewer than 4 each.

We use data from Denison for both shares and inputs.[24] These are given in Table B.4. The basic estimation is obtained by taking the logarithms of (B.9).

$$\ln z = A + \rho \left[\ln \left(\frac{N}{R} \right) + \lambda t \right] \qquad \text{(B.10)}$$

where A is a constant. N is calculated from (B.8), taking ϵ equal to 0.242 from Table B.1 above.

$$\ln z = 1.797 - .5046 \ln (N/R) - .0319t \qquad R^2 = .9816 \qquad \text{(B.11)}$$
$$(0.026) \quad (.3486) \qquad\qquad (.0169) \qquad SE = .026$$

This regression implies an elasticity of substitution between neo-classical factors and resources of about 2 and a value of λ of 0.06. It

[24] One should give the usual caveats about the data. The labor and capital figures are probably good, but Denison assumes that inputs of natural resources are constant due to the domination of land in natural resource inputs. Since the nonland component in resources has certainly been rising, we understate the growth of R, and consequently we probably overstate ρ.

TABLE B.4
Factor Inputs
(*1929 = 100;*
in each period, resources equal
100.0 on the 1929 base)

	Capital	Labor
1909–13	57.28	67.58
1914–18	65.48	76.10
1919–23	77.00	79.32
1924–28	90.94	92.12
1929–33	101.60	88.74
1934–38	99.44	95.76
1939–43	106.36	132.06
1944–48	114.28	154.14
1949–53	136.92	160.68
1954–58	162.30	174.40

Source: Denison, *Sources,* pp. 85 and 100.

is consistent with the general impression given by the simulation tests — either the elasticity of substitution is high or technological change is relatively resource-saving or both.

APPENDIX C: POPULATION GROWTH AND SUSTAINABLE CONSUMPTION

Equilibrium or Intrinsic Population Growth

A population is in equilibrium when the number of persons of any given age and sex increases at the same percentage rate year after year. This constant rate is the same for all age-sex classes, and therefore for the aggregate size of the population and for the numbers of births and deaths. In equilibrium the relative age-sex composition of the population remains constant.

Such an equilibrium will generally be reached asymptotically if the fertility and mortality structure of the population remains constant. Mortality structure means the vector of death rates by age and sex. Fertility structure means the vector of male and female births as a proportion of the female population of various ages. The equilibrium rate of growth of a population and its equilibrium age distribution will be different for different fertility and mortality structures.

The net reproduction rate, for a given fertility and mortality structure, is the average number of females who will be born to a female baby during her lifetime. For zero population growth (ZPG) this rate must be 1.000. When it is higher, the equilibrium rate of population growth per year will depend also on how early or late in life the average female gives birth.

In the text three equilibrium populations are compared, one corresponding to the 1960 fertility and mortality structure, one to the 1967 structure, and one to an assumed ZPG structure. The 1960 and 1967 structures were obtained from the U.S. Census. The ZPG estimates use the 1967 mortality structure, and a fertility vector obtained by proportionately scaling down the 1967 vector enough to obtain a net reproduction rate of 1.000. Figure C.1 shows the three vectors of birth rates by age of woman: 1960, 1967, ZPG.

The differences in equilibrium age distribution associated with differences in fertility structure are illustrated in Figures C.2, C.3, and C.4. These figures also show actual age distributions for 1960 and 1967. The differences between actual and equilibrium age distributions are, of course, responsible for the considerable discrepancies between actual and equilibrium rates of population growth.

Finally, Figures C.5, C.6, and C.7, show for each of the three structures (a) the hypothetical "projection" which the population would follow if the fertility-mortality structure remained constant, given the initial disequilibrium, and (b) the "constant rate" equilibrium path to which the projected path would converge.

These calculations make no allowance for net immigration, which amounts to 300,000 to 400,000 persons per year under current legislation.

Life Cycle Saving and Aggregate Wealth

As explained in the text, the effect of a change in the equilibrium rate of population growth on sustainable consumption depends in part on the change in the stock of wealth the society desires to hold relative to its income. We have taken the "life cycle" approach to this problem, as described in Tobin's paper "Life Cycle Saving and Balanced Growth." [25]

[25] In *Ten Economic Studies in the Tradition of Irving Fisher,* ed. William Fellner, New York, Wiley, 1967, pp. 231–56.

FIGURE C.1
Actual U.S. Birth Rates, 1960 and 1967, and Rates Assuming Zero
Population Growth (ZPG)

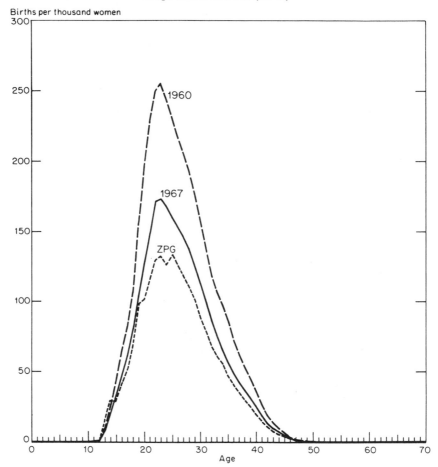

The population is assumed to be in equilibrium, and the calculations have been made for the three fertility-mortality structures already
described: 1960, 1967, ZPG. It is necessary further to group the populations in households. This is done arbitrarily by associating with each
female 18 or older: (a) her pro rata share of the living males two years
older, and (b) all the surviving children ever born to an average female
of her age. Males are children until 20, females until 18; at those ages

FIGURE C.2
Actual 1960 Age Distribution and Equilibrium Distribution of the
U.S. Female Population

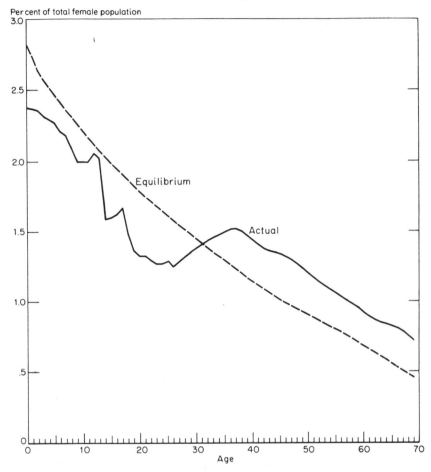

they create new households. Over the life of a household its average size varies as births and deaths occur.

The household's income each year is the sum of the incomes of its various members. These vary with age and sex, according to profiles published by the Census Bureau and based on the Current Population Survey. The 1960 profile was used with the 1960 demographic structure, the 1967 profile with the 1967 and ZPG structures. The whole

FIGURE C.3
Actual 1967 Age Distribution and Equilibrium Distribution of the
U.S. Female Population

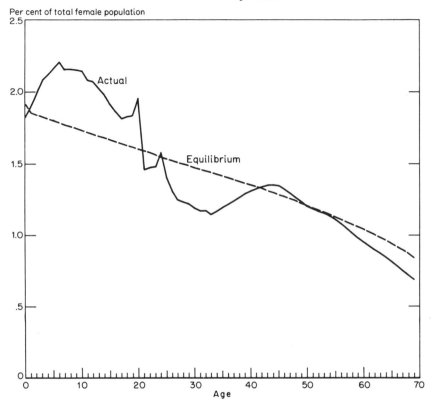

profile is assumed to shift upward at 3 per cent per year, the assumed
rate of increase of productivity due to labor-augmenting technological
progress. Labor inputs of different ages and sexes are assumed to be
perfect substitutes, at rates indicated by the profiles.

Each household is assumed to know its future size, n, its labor income, y and the interest rate, r. Over its lifetime the average household
consumes all of its income, including interest on any savings accumu-
lated along the way. The household spreads its consumption more
evenly than its income, saving in high-income years in order to dissave
in low-income years. The utility, u, of consumption at any time is taken
to be a function of the consumption, c, per surviving equivalent adult

FIGURE C.4

Actual 1967 Age Distribution and ZPG Equilibrium Distribution of
U.S. Female Population

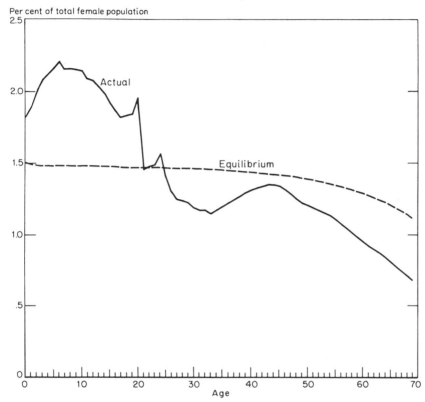

member of the household at that time. The household maximizes over
its lifetime the sum of the utilities of this consumption at each age, a,
weighted by the expected number of equivalent adult members in the
household at that age, $n(a)$, discounted by a subjective rate of time
preference, ρ: $\int e^{-\rho a} u[c(a)]n(a)da$, where the limits of integration are
from $a = 0$ to $a = A$. This is maximized subject to the budget constraint
that expected lifetime income equals expected lifetime consumption:

$$Y = \int e^{-ra} y(a)da = \int e^{-ra} c(a)n(a)da$$

where the integration limits are the same as before and where $y(a)$ is
the expected labor income of a household at age a. The calculations

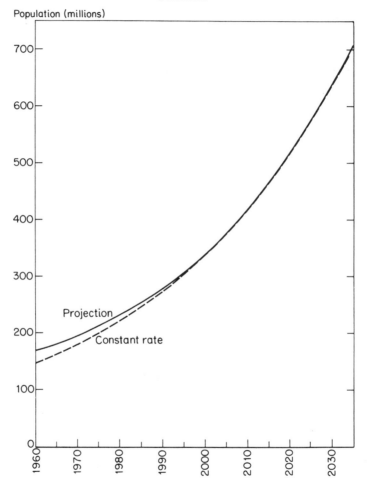

FIGURE C.5
Projected and Equilibrium U.S. Population, 1960 Fertility-Mortality
Structure

have been made for the specific utility function $u(c) = \ln c$. This leads
to the following rule:

$$c(a) = \frac{e^{(r-\rho)a}Y}{\int e^{-\rho a}n(a)da}$$

where the limits of integration are the same as before; Y is the present
value, at household age 0, of its expected lifetime labor income; and

FIGURE C.6
Projected and Equilibrium U.S. Population, 1967 Fertility-Mortality
Structure

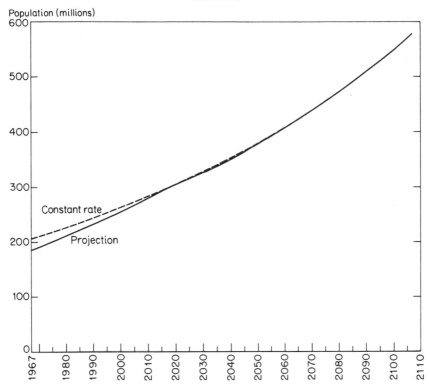

the denominator is the discounted sum of expected equivalent adult years of household life and consumption. If the market and subjective discount rates were equal, the rule says that lifetime income should be spread evenly in consumption, so that consumption per equivalent adult would be constant. To the extent that r exceeds ρ the household is induced to postpone consumption until later in life.

As this exposition makes clear, the household's consumption pattern depends on (a) the way in which its members are counted—the equivalent adult scale, and (b) the subjective discount rate. Calculations have been made for various equivalent adult scales, ranging from counting teenagers and other children as full members to counting them not at all. In one case the parents are diminishing their old-age consumption in order to increase household consumption during the

FIGURE C.7
Projected and Equilibrium U.S. Population for ZPG Fertility-Mortality
Structure

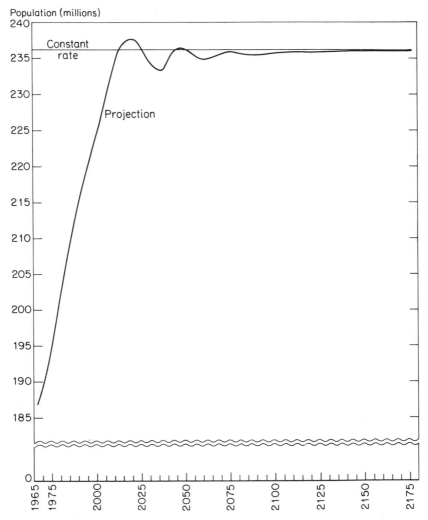

years children are at home; in the other case they are not. Likewise a
number of values of subjective discount rate have been assumed. Some
of the combinations are shown in text Tables 2–4. For the present purpose, which is to exhibit the effects of changes in the fertility-mortality
structure, the assumed equivalent adult scales and subjective discount

rate matter very little. They would matter if they were thought to vary systematically with the rate of population growth, but there is no reason to expect that.

On the other hand, the response of consumption patterns to market interest rates does matter. It is this response that makes the aggregate wealth-income ratio respond to market interest rates, as illustrated in the upward sloping curves of text Figure 1.

Household consumption planning is assumed to be actuarial. A given cohort of households breaks even over its lifetime. Some households last longer than average, and some dwindle away sooner. Life insurance and annuities enable the excess consumption of some members of a cohort to be met by the excess saving of other members.

Similarly, households are assumed to be able to borrow, as well as lend, at will at the prevailing interest rate, so long as they have expected future labor income to borrow against. This assumption of a perfect capital market has less effect than might have been supposed, because in most cases households have few or no years of negative net worth.

Given the consumption plan of an average household, it is possible to compute at any time the number, the net worth positions, and the income of households of every age. From this the aggregate wealth-income ratio can be computed. Along a path of equilibrium population and economic growth this ratio will be a constant, dependent on the characteristics of the path but unchanging over time. The reasons that it is a constant of this kind are essentially that (a) the lifetime propensity to consume equals unity regardless of the absolute size of income, and (b) all the demographic and economic variables that determine the pattern of consumption of a household over its lifetime, and the age distribution of households and their members, are constant along an equilibrium path.

As indicated in text Tables 4–6, the key economic variable, the interest rate, is identified with the net marginal productivity of capital and depends on the capital-output ratio. Here we have also made the capital-output ratio and the wealth-income ratio identical. This would not be the case if we allowed for accumulation of wealth in forms other than capital.[26] Then the two ratios would differ, but our conclusions about the effects of population growth would not be affected so long as

[26] See James Tobin, "Money and Economic Growth," *Econometrica*, October 1965, pp. 671–84; and Tobin, "Notes on Optimal Monetary Growth," *Journal of Political Economy*, August 1968, pp. 833–59.

the monetary-fiscal policies that determine the difference remained the same.

How does the fertility-mortality structure affect the aggregate wealth-income ratio? The most obvious way is that it determines the equilibrium age distribution. For example, ZPG puts relatively more households in the retirement years, when wealth declines to zero. On the other hand, it also puts more households in the high-wealth years just before retirement, and fewer in the early, low-wealth years. A less obvious effect is the life cycle of household size. With ZPG, there are fewer children to claim consumption as against the retirement consumption of the adults. When children are counted in the consumption plan, therefore, ZPG raises the peak wealth accumulations of middle-aged households. The upshot is, as reported in text Tables 4–6 and Figure 1, that reduction in fertility raises aggregate wealth-income ratios at all interest rates.

DISCUSSION

Includes comments by R. Aaron Gordon, a member of the Board of Directors of the National Bureau of Economic Research and professor at the University of California at Berkeley, who was moderator of this session; and by Moses Abramovitz, also a member of the National Bureau's Board of Directors and professor at Stanford University, and Robin C. O. Matthews, professor at All Souls College, who acted as program discussants. The recorded oral presentations were edited by, or with the cooperation of, the speakers. Remarks made during the open discussion period are not included.

Introductory Remarks by R. Aaron Gordon

This is the fifth in a series of six colloquia commemorating the fiftieth anniversary of the founding of the National Bureau of Economic Research, a private, nonprofit research organization which has made an indelible mark on empirical research in the field of economics. The first of these colloquia, held much earlier this year, dealt with the subject of business cycles, with the subject of the cumulative instability of the American and other advanced economies. But short-run instability is closely related to the question of the long-run dynamics of the system, specifically to the subject of economic growth. Until very recently economists concerned themselves with the dynamics of the growth process and with the problem of how to stimulate growth further. But now the question is being asked: Why economic growth? Do the quantitative measures that economists and statisticians have created over the last quarter century or more really measure the benefits to society of steadily increasing output? By your or my criteria, what is the effect of economic growth on social welfare? This next to last of our colloquia deals with this question: What is growth, what do we get out of it, and, to quote the title of the main paper presented to us, is economic growth obsolete? Do we really want growth as much as we thought we did? This is the subject of today's colloquium.

* * *

Moses Abramovitz: The very least that one needs to say about the paper by Jim Tobin and Bill Nordhaus is that it opens up almost all of the subjects that have intrigued economists for a very long period of time. Not only how to measure the growth of economic welfare, but also what the relation is between growth of economic welfare and actual resources on one side and population growth on the other side. Having had the opportunity to read the text of the paper, I was especially interested in the very opening sentences, and if I may, I would like to read them to you:

"A long decade ago economic growth was the reigning fashion of political economy. It was simultaneously the hottest subject of economic theory and research, a slogan eagerly claimed by politicians of all stripes, and the serious objective of the policies of governments. The climate of opinion has changed dramatically."

As we heard in the paper presented to us, this is followed by a series of remarks on the current disenchantment with economic growth. The feeling that I picked up in reading the paper was that the authors not only resist that disenchantment, a resistance with which I associate myself at least in a qualified way, but that they are also surprised that this feeling of disenchantment should have arisen.

I think it is of some interest to say at the very outset that a long decade ago not all economists shared in the reigning fashion. There were at least some economists who even at that time were looking skeptically at what it was that we thought we would be getting out of a high rate of growth, given the kinds of uses to which output was being put. For example, in 1958, which, I guess, qualifies as a long decade ago, the CED published a series of essays in which the question posed to the contributors was, What do you regard as the most important economic problem of the next generation? As one might have predicted, essays on a great many subjects appeared in that volume. Some six or eight of them were directed to questioning the value of economic growth, having regard to the way product was then being used. And not all of those essayists were the predictable ones. Galbraith was certainly one of them, but so was the first winner of the Nobel Prize for Economic Science, Jan Tinbergen, as well as, ironically enough, the father of modern economic growth, Roy Harrod. The complaint of these essayists was not so much that economic growth as properly measured had ceased, or even that it had become slow, but that growth was being misdirected; that private consumption was being more and more devoted to trivial uses. They saw serious reasons why a continued attempt to absorb increased amounts of income into private consumption would prove frustrating to people seeking a rise in their level of satisfaction. They worried about a neglect of the needs for public overhead in the cities and elsewhere, and about the need to regulate private activities that had important side effects. They worried about the underdevelopment of public services that had a broad significance for the country—for example, education and health. They were concerned with the neglect of the distributive aspects of our income flow, and they were disappointed and concerned about the failure to make a more vigorous effort to use American wealth for people in poorer countries. One of these essays concluded with the following sentences:

"If we must risk some reduction in our rate of growth in order to apply our expanded capacity to more worthy, meaningful uses, it is a risk well worthwhile. If we refuse to accept it we may discover that the economic progress of the next generation was an empty achievement, not only in the eyes of people in other countries, but perhaps still more in our own."[1]

I take it that this prediction of disenchantment is at least partially confirmed by the kind of public discussion with which we are all familiar. Now, in facing the present disenchantment, it seems to me that questions of two sorts arise: First of all, what was the true long-term growth rate of income, and second, what is it worth, and what kinds of risks are worth taking with growth in order to promote other goals, or to make the actual growth, whatever it is, more valuable to us? In approaching these two questions, it is perfectly clear that Nordhaus and Tobin have focused on the first of these questions. They recognize, as we all do, that conventional estimates of national product are neither completely comprehensive nor completely consistent and accurate measures of output relevant to welfare. They attempt a revision, and, in the course of doing so, take a swing at almost all the problems—you might almost call them classical problems—of national income accounting. They take a swing at all of them, or perhaps all but one of them, and they conclude that the sustainable growth rate of our output of the goods that count for welfare was, if anything, somewhat higher than the conventional measures suggest. So the general message is that the economy, though subject to improvement, has been churning out, even in its present imperfect state, final consumer goods or sources of welfare, or their equivalent in leisure, at a substantial rate of growth. And this, they say, is as far as economists can possibly carry the debate over the grounds of our present disenchantment.

Although in a sense the paper is clearly intended to be a contribu-

[1] Moses Abramovitz, "Economic Goals and Social Welfare in the Next Generation," in *Problems of U.S. Economic Development*, Committee for Economic Development, New York, 1958, pp. 191–99.

tion to the debate over the value of growth for policy, we probably ought to recognize, as Tobin and Nordhaus certainly do, that the revision of our national accounts has a complementary goal (which may be the more important goal of the paper) — to stimulate economists to renew work on the improvement of our national product estimates, to make them more useful as a basis for the study of growth and for judgments about its value. In that sense the Tobin-Nordhaus procedures are more important than their conclusions. I shall have very little to say about the sections of their paper that deal with the possible over-exploitation of national resources or population growth. In part, that's because I think I agree with those portions of their paper so far as I understand them, and in part it is because I really haven't had a chance to absorb all of those sections. I might venture one comment on what they have to say about population. Part of the reassurance that they give us with respect to the question of population growth rests on the present low level to which the standardized fertility rates have sunk during the last five or six, or perhaps eight or ten, years. Some of the best work on fertility trends in recent years, however, runs to the conclusion that these movements are themselves sensitive to economic conjunctures. In particular, it appears that marriage and birth rates depend on the economic status and prospects of young adults. When the population of young adults is growing slowly and the demand for labor is urgent, the economic fortunes of young people are favorable. They marry early, they have more children and have them sooner. In the opposing conjuncture, which seemed to rule during the decade immediately past, fertility rates fall. As many of you know, I am merely repeating the outcome of Richard Easterlin's work. The possibility arises, therefore, that just as the very high birth rates of the forties and early fifties have proved to be a transient characteristic of our economy, the lower birth rates we're witnessing today may also turn out to be transient, and we may find ourselves some years from now worrying again about higher levels of fertility.

Let me make just a few points about the new measure of economic welfare which Tobin and Nordhaus are proposing to us. I must say, right off, that I agree almost entirely with the spirit of the revisions they are proposing. When viewed as a set of challenges to take the first steps toward including in our national accounts things we have unjustifiably omitted in the past and excluding from the accounts matters that, we've always recognized, ought to be excluded from a long-term point of view, the paper is, I think, going to leave a very important mark on the statistical and economic work of the next years. With many of their proposals I'm wholly in agreement. I agree, of course, that for almost all purposes we want to have per capita measures, not aggregates, and I agree that our basic concern ought to be with the levels and growth of consumption or its equivalent. I agree also that, if possible, we ought to measure growth not from the observed values but from estimates of the sustainable levels of consumption. This means that we're entitled to add what one may call the true net capital formation to consumption. But, that true net capital formation must be measured after accounting for all capital stock obligations, and that means, in particular, one capital stock obligation on which Tobin and Nordhaus put stress, namely, the obligation to take care, in some sense, of additions to the population. We have to include not only enough capital to make good conventional depreciation but also to outfit new workers with the same level of capital equipment as old workers. In addition, and here's the rub, we must fit them with enough capital to keep technological progress going forward at established rates. But there is, of course, a murky area, as Bill Nordhaus described it to us. The position they have adopted is that the additional capital that must be set aside before, so to speak, we feel entitled to consume anything is one which they compute on an assumption consistent with the requirements for constant growth in a steady state. This is that no technological progress be of a sort that economizes on capital. It's all, as the phrase goes, labor-augmenting. I must say, I find it hard at first blush to feel that many people are going to be comfortable about the proposition that we must make a commitment to some specified but unverified quality of technological change in setting up our national accounts. The other implication of this new concept of depreciation, or capital obligations, is that it's our duty to endow our children, not with the same level of economic welfare that we enjoy, but with the same rate of growth in economic welfare. If, as appears to be the case, the level of economic welfare now seems to be doubling every thirty years, we have the obligation to insure that our children should be twice as well off as we are.

Turning to another subject, let me say a word about their treatment of the hoary and touchy question of regrettable necessities. In arriving at the consumption that is relevant to welfare, Tobin and Nordhaus would exclude both the output of intermediate goods and the provision for what they call regrettable necessities, particularly for defense expenditures. Now, I'm not absolutely sure whether we have a difference in principle here or not. I would not view measures of output relevant to economic welfare as intended to answer the question, "Are we better off than in the past, and by how much?" but to answer the question, "What is the contribution of our economic activity to making us better off than we were in the past?" And if, therefore, needs arise from conditions which are not themselves tied to our economic activity and if we have to divert resources to satisfying those needs, one ought not to say that the contribution of our economic activity to welfare has been less than it was if those needs had not arisen. With respect to the treatment of defense expenditures, we need to ask ourselves why such expenditures have increased. Has the need the country seems to feel for diverting resources to that purpose arisen as a result of the economic activity in which we're engaged or has it arisen for other reasons? If one concludes, as I think one must, that the need has other reasons, there would be little excuse for excluding defense expenditures from a measure of output relevant to welfare.

Bill Nordhaus has told us that a major reason why their new revision indicates that the growth rate of economic welfare has been, if anything, somewhat higher than conventional measures suggest, is that the value of leisure has been growing very rapidly. Looking at these figures, my first instinct was to think that the growth rate of leisure for purposes of national income accounting was greatly exaggerated. The more I thought about it, however, the more confused I became over the subject, and it wasn't until Robin Matthews arrived a couple of days ago that I was able to get straightened out. I now believe that those figures are greatly exaggerated, but that, in a sense, is his story and I'm going to leave it to him to tell it to you.

Finally, a word on this question of disamenities. I think it ought to be clear that the measure of the burden of disamenities, up to the point to which Nordhaus and Tobin are able to take it in the present paper, is necessarily incomplete. It takes into account only the results of the structural shift of the population toward higher levels of concentration and leaves out of account the possible increase in the burden which has arisen in communities of all sizes. We know that the population in the central cities of the country has not been growing in the last twenty years. Yet we all have the strong feeling that life in those cities has become more difficult. If that's so, and if the earnings differentials between cities of different sizes have remained stable, the clear suggestion is that the difficulties of life, of communal life if you like, have been increasing for reasons other than the shift of population to larger urban communities. That's one reason for the incompleteness of their measure. The other is that sources of disamenities that are unrelated to the size of the communities in which people reside are not included in their estimates.

Mr. Chairman, the subject invites extended discussion. I think the only way to conclude what I have to say while this audience is still here is to sit down.

Robin C. O. Matthews: What Tobin and Nordhaus have done in their impressive paper is to put into the context of modern growth theory and to clothe with statistical apparel concepts most of which had been the subject of discussion by economists long before growth became one of our central concepts.

Systematic treatment of the relation between economic welfare and national income measures began with Pigou and was revived in the debates on welfare economics in the 1940s. Those debates were concerned with two types of issues, both of them relevant to the discussion of today's paper. The first type of issue was of a broad philosophical kind, about the dimensions of economic welfare (or welfare in general) and about the propriety of using any variant of national income measure to gauge it. The second type of issue was more technical, largely about index numbers. I will come back to the philosophical aspect presently.

The index number problem is apparent most acutely in connection with the valuation of time devoted to nonmarket activity. The essence of the index number problem is that we don't know the appropriate weights (prices) to give to the different elements entering into an aggregate. For the evaluation of nonmarket time, Tobin and Nordhaus offer two extreme alternatives, together with a preferred compromise. The pessimistic alternative is to treat an hour of nonworking time as a final good and value it at its price, the hourly wage rate. This has the effect of causing MEW to rise less rapidly than consumption, so long as nonmarket time rises less rapidly than consumption, as it does. The optimistic alternative is to treat an hour of nonworking time as a means of producing final goods, and to assume that the rise in the marginal product of working time, as measured by the rise in the hourly wage rate, has been matched by an equal rise in the marginal product of the multifarious activities to which nonmarket time can be devoted. These activities range from do-it-yourself in the production of final goods that could alternatively be bought in the market at the one extreme to activities that you *have* to do yourself, like sleeping, on the other. The effect of the optimistic procedure is, broadly speaking, to solve the problem of how to weight changes in working time and changes in consumption by substituting the hourly real wage for the more usual measure of the annual real wage (with appropriate allowance for profits, etc.).

Since much more of life is spent in nonmarket activities than in market activities, the valuation of nonmarket time comes out as by far the largest constituent of total MEW. The way it is handled dominates the result and completely swamps refinements made elsewhere in the measure. I imagine Tobin and Nordhaus intended this part of their exercise as an illustration of possible results rather than as something they would actually recommend for statistical practice. The choice of valuation to be placed both on leisure and on nonmarket work is bound to be largely arbitrary, as is the division of nonmarket time between these two categories. This is surely a case, therefore, where it is best to recognize that a basis of valuation is so completely lacking that the attempt at aggregation should be abandoned. Fortunately, we know that hours of work have fallen over time, so making an allowance for them is not going to alter the *direction* of change of MEW; and we are not going to be able to put any faith in measures of their effect on the *extent* of change in MEW. So we do best to fall back on a vector – as is done by the compilers of social indicators. We can just say that over a given period there has been such and such an increase in consumption and such and such a change in the number of working hours. And we can usefully supplement this by saying that the change in the number of working hours has been due to such and such an extent to changes in the normal working week, to changes in holidays, and to changes in participation rates of students, old people, and married women, all of which may obviously have quite different welfare implications.

Similar issues, in some ways more intractable, arise in an element of economic welfare hardly touched on by Tobin and Nordhaus, namely, conditions of work. Over time there has clearly been a major improvement in conditions of work. Whether the improvement has been proportionately greater or less than in consumption per head we don't know. Good conditions of work are something on which workers set a high valuation, as evidenced by the prominent place it occupies in claims made by labor unions. The failure to take account of changes in conditions of work in conventional national income measures is particularly gross, because some of the goods and services that enter into conditions of work are actually the same as those that are included in ordinary consumption measures, such as space heating and the use of furniture. It is obviously ridiculous to maintain that warmth or a comfortable chair contributes to economic welfare if it is enjoyed at home but not if it is enjoyed in the office. I admit it is not clear what one should do about this. One possibility would be to take a few clearly defined items like those I have just mentioned and put them into measures of national product. This would leave out of account the more intangible, and possibly more important, things affecting the conditions of work, such as its arduousness, its social environment, and so on. One could imagine, in theory at least, a calculation rather like the one done by Tobin and Nordhaus about the disamenities of urbanization. One could compare different occupations on the principle of equal net advantages, note that these different occupations have attached to them different amounts of the various elements that constitute good conditions of work, and thereby calculate a hedonic price index for each of the elements, finally using these prices to give a measure of the value over time of the increase in welfare contributed by the improvement in the various elements. This would obviously be a difficult undertaking for many reasons. But it is quite an important matter, and in some ways it is really worse than the problem of hours of work, because with hours of work there is a single measure you can fall back on — the number of hours worked — whereas in the case of conditions of work there is no single measure available, let alone any means of combining it with consumption in an aggregate measure of MEW.

I pass now to a different point. The subject chosen by Tobin and Nordhaus gives their paper inevitably a different orientation from the mainstream of work on economic growth. Most of this work is about the causes of growth rather than its measurement or desirability. To what extent are these fields of study connected? Moses Abramovitz has called attention to one connection between the two in his remarks about the model of technical change implicit in the treatment of widening investment in the paper before us. Let me mention a couple of other connections.

The first concerns population growth. The neoclassical model says that if you compare two countries with different rates of population growth, the country with a 1 per cent faster rate of population growth will have a 1 per cent faster rate of growth of output in the steady state. This is what is assumed in the part of the paper of Tobin and Nordhaus where they are discussing the consequences of alternative rates of population growth. It seems to be broadly confirmed by the statistical studies of Kuznets and Deborah Paige, who found no particular relationship between the rate of growth of population and the rate of growth of income per head in the long run in a comparison between different countries. It is curious, however, that within the postwar period a comparison of countries leads to a different result. Very little correlation is found between the rate of growth of population in different countries and the rate of growth of their *total* national income. It is not sensible to expect to find one-to-one correlations all the time, and this finding may be no more than accidental. But if it persisted for a long period one might perhaps have to reconsider some of the fundamentals of this sort of model and, in particular, its almost total emphasis on supply considerations as opposed to demand considerations in the determination of the rate of growth. We have not yet established a satisfactory reconciliation between the theory underlying the two classic topics of National Bureau research, growth and business cycles.

There is also a connection between the desirability of growth and the causes of growth. In discussing possible ways in which growth may be undesirable, Tobin and Nordhaus direct their attention mainly to the various *consequences* of growth. But economic growth itself is the result of many different forces, and it is extremely plausible to suppose that some of these forces involve disamenities to a greater extent than others. All economic growth admittedly involves change, and change is disturbing, but some kinds of change are more disturbing than others. So understanding the causes of economic growth, in different countries and different periods, is relevant to assessing its desirability.

My final point about the relation between the causes of economic growth and the subject of the present paper is this. As a British guest at this colloquium, I am conscious that Tobin and Nordhaus are concerned with *American* economic growth and what they say is not necessarily intended for export. There are indeed certain points where the paper seems to me to have a distinctively American orientation. I am not thinking simply of the point that developing countries are not on any reckoning threatened with overly rapid growth—although that does perhaps require to be said in the context of this sort of discussion from time to time. A more special form of American orientation in the paper seems to me to come in the authors' statement that policy for fast growth, insofar as it isn't just stabilization policy dressed up, amounts to a policy of high saving in one form or another. This may be true the way growth policy has been understood here. But in Europe and also in developing countries it has commonly been supposed that the promotion of growth includes as a major element in policy the inducement of changes in attitudes and changes in social relationships. It would be artificial to describe these as changes in saving. Their effects on welfare are obviously very difficult for economists to measure. But insofar as the promotion of such changes is a part of growth policy, the evaluation of their consequences is part of the evaluation of the policy.

In conclusion I revert to the philosophical class of questions that were raised in the discussions of the new welfare economics in the 1940s. A key point in welfare theory established in that debate — reaffirming what had been said by Pigou — was that the concept of income (or consumption) is to be distinguished from the concept of economic welfare. Economic welfare depends not only on the size of the national income but on its distribution. So I think MEW is not the right description of what Tobin and Nordhaus are measuring — it is a measure of consumption, not a measure of welfare. The distribution of income is another term that has to go into the welfare vector along with sustainable consumption per head, hours of work, and possibly some others. This is a verbal point. A more substantial one concerns our relation with other disciplines. In the paper before us the authors write, "We can't go beyond a certain point and this is the point where economic welfare becomes identified with subjective well-being or happiness or contentment. In measuring these ultimates and their correlation with things economic, we pass the baton to the philosophers and the psychologists."[2] This sort of remark is also often made by people who are writing about the *causes* of economic growth. It is made with the unspoken implication, sometimes the spoken implication, that although we pass the baton to psychologists or sociologists, it's extremely probable that they'll drop it or run in the wrong direction with it, but there's nothing much we can do about it. I suppose that most economists, if pressed, wouldn't really advocate such a rigid division of labor between the social sciences in considering either the causes of economic growth or its consequences. It would be difficult to defend it because, after all, economic welfare is not a special kind of welfare, it's a special means of procuring welfare, and even so not easy to define in a distinctive way. But in practice such relationship as there has been between disciplines has been largely in the area of applied work. It

[2] In the final version of the paper this passage does not appear. But the thought remains, so I have allowed my comment to stand.

hasn't affected the theoretical structure of economics at all, and hence it hasn't affected the way in which we pose questions. I think the trouble is we don't take pains to state in terms appropriate to other disciplines the problems we expect them to solve. In fact, worse, we sometimes beg questions that lie properly in their department. For example, I think that there is some substance in the charge that the mainstream of economic theory depends on the psychological assumptions of Jeremy Bentham. And if present-day psychologists reject Benthamite psychology, it's not a promising approach to interdisciplinary cooperation to say to psychologists: "Here are the conclusions on the economic aspects of the question, based on postulates you reject, now please supplement these by telling us the conclusions on the noneconomic postulates." The cooperation between ourselves and other social scientists should begin at an earlier stage.

*   *   *

Closing Remarks by R. Aaron Gordon

It would appear at this stage of the proceedings that growth *does* matter, and that, even when the welfare implications of growth are taken into account, despite some protest to the contrary, we are somehow better off than we were, at least in 1929.